"Thank you, I love you God, creator of everything."

Dan Roach

God

God

Dan Roach

Columbus, Ohio

This book is a work of fiction. The names, characters and events in this book are the products of the author's imagination or are used fictitiously. Any similarity to real persons living or dead is coincidental and not intended by the author.

The views and opinions expressed in this book are solely those of the author and do not reflect the views or opinions of Gatekeeper Press. Gatekeeper Press is not to be held responsible for and expressly disclaims responsibility of the content herein.

God

Published by Gatekeeper Press
2167 Stringtown Rd, Suite 109
Columbus, OH 43123-2989
www.GatekeeperPress.com

Copyright © 2021 by Dan Roach
All rights reserved. Neither this book, nor any parts within it may be sold or reproduced in any form or by any electronic or mechanical means, including information storage and retrieval systems, without permission in writing from the author. The only exception is by a reviewer, who may quote short excerpts in a review.

The interior formatting, typesetting, and editorial work for this book are entirely the product of the author. Gatekeeper Press did not participate in and is not responsible for any aspect of these elements.

ISBN (paperback): 9781662914287

The title of this book is *GOD* and God wants to get your attention. He always has wanted to get your attention.

We all know there is a mystery when it comes to creation and life. Do you think about it much? Why should people care about all of this? We should care because the signs point to a creator, God. He has been trying to help us. Why? It is simple. He created us and loves us. God doesn't want to lose any of us. God said He gave us free will, so we have to choose God. We have to acknowledge God and love Him back.

Most scientists and professors want us to believe that everything we see just kind of popped up. God gave us the Bible to let us know certain things, like creation didn't just pop up. Scientists want us to believe that a "big bang" in empty space and the universe started that way. We don't get "big bangs" from nothing (empty space). Scientists will say they can tell there are "big bangs" occasionally, and they make new stars and planets. Well, there is a lot in space now, gases, debris, and etc. It was completely empty with the first "big bang" and they know that. They really have no good answers.

I read something a man said that I liked about the 'big bang". He said the "big bang" scientists talk about would be like throwing a grenade into a forest and getting furniture. A "big bang" or explosion would cause lots of chaos and debris would go everywhere. We are smart enough to know that.

However the universe started, it was set up perfectly for life on this planet. If the first "big bang" did happen, there was only one thing that could do it in empty space, and that would be God. He could have used a "big bang", but I believe He just willed the universe to happen, and it did. He also knew exactly where the sun and the rest of the planets would be set up.

In writing this book I learned more about how the planets and the universe were set up for life on this planet. For one thing, the earth, the sun, and the moon needed to be the right size. That would have to do with gravity, and the sun of course needed to be the right distance from earth. To think about creation and how perfect it was, and needed to be, you have to think about God. Most scientists and professors like to figure creation by science and leave God out. You have to get into strange things about creation, leaving God out. The earth needed to have an atmosphere to block off a lot of the sun's harmful rays. Something else the earth has that I know little about is a magnetic field. The magnetic field blocks off gamma rays and gamma particles from the sun. These gamma rays and particles can be deadly. The earth has an inner iron core and molten iron around the core that is revolving. This causes the magnetic field, all around the earth. If we didn't have this, we would not be able to live with our sun, and I'm sure that puts it gently. How this creation was set up so perfectly, took God to know how to do it. Scientists at least will say they don't know for sure. How could they know? Well, this is the point where I say shame on many scientists and professors. If you leave God out, things like ape to man, the "big bang" and other things stick. Because of so called intelligent people, things are taught in our schools that are wrong. By the way it is also the point where I mention Satan. Satan doesn't want us believing in God at all.

Creation just goes on and on, and only God could create it all. Only God could think of everything needed for life on earth.

The earth is traveling around the sun at approximately 67,000 miles per hour and at the right distance. The earth rotates as it moves, giving us night and day. It takes a year to completely circle the sun. We get our seasons by the tilt of the earth towards the sun. We also have that oversized moon that revolves around the earth as we revolve around the sun. This is exciting, and interesting stuff. We have heard some about our moon, like the effects on ocean waves and tides. I didn't realize the agitation of the ocean waves, and tides keep stagnation from happening. I heard the moon also has a gravitational effect on earth as we fly around the sun. The earth tends to wobble a little, and the moon helps to prevent that. I would just say God is amazing how He created things.

If you think of all creation, and how things were set up for life, a person could write many books about it. Just thinking about creation and studying some about it I am amazed. It points straight to a Creator, God. Since we all were born, and creation was already here we take it all for granted. We also take the Bible for granted, being that it has been around forever, it seems. So, do we take God for granted? I think most people on this planet don't' think much about this invisible God. Maybe God is like the wind, we can't see it, but it is there. All through history humans have had a problem with an invisible God. The Bible tells us that God is spirit, and God is not human.

Before the Bible, God dealt with His creation more hands on you could say. He gave the Hebrews (Jews) the Ten Commandments to help them know what He wanted of them. God is a perfect being, and that is what He wants and expects in His creation. Well everyone on this planet, even being created in God's image, are not at all like God. That is because we are all sinners. Bad things, hate, evil, and just all sins go completely against this God of ours. It is very interesting to me. It is like in a nutshell, God originally created everything perfect, and in the end that is exactly what He is going to have.

Being that God is perfect, and a God of love and mercy, that I think is why people are still here today. God had to fix the problem of sin, and He did. Just like the original creation was perfect, God's plan to save the world, from sin was perfect. It took His Son, Jesus to come, and live as a man on this earth and do what had to be done. We don't fully understand, but that is why God gave us the Bible.

Jesus, also being God never sinned, but gave up His life willingly for us humans. He took all sin on Himself and was ridiculed, spit on, beat on, whipped and then crucified. That was Jesus' mission, or the plan of God the Father, and Jesus did it. To Christians it is sad, but also wonderful what Jesus did. If He didn't do it there would be no way for any human, as sinners to be with a perfect God. God the Father brought Jesus back to life, and we can follow Jesus. That was the perfect plan. Does that mean we have to be perfect like Jesus? We can only believe and accept the free gift from God. As for us being perfect we can only pray for forgiveness. So, do you think about this loving God that we have? Being that He is perfect and holy, and pretty much everything we are not, He wants us, His creation to live with Him for eternity. That is what it is all about now. Jesus did what had to be done, but on this world of ours we still have a problem with sin. God has a foe and he is low down, an angel that went bad, Lucifer or Satan. Satan actually wants to keep people from the salvation Jesus offers, and God the Father. God wants us to be with Him, so Satan will do everything he can to keep that from happening. I know we have a mystery, but isn't this world and us a mystery? An example of what Satan does is ape to man. Man evolved from an ape like creature, no way! Like God didn't create, it just popped up from a "big bang" in empty space. This sort of stuff is in our schools, and our museums. Natural science museums where you see dinosaur bones, also show giant posters of ape to man. The greatest liar, and deceiver should be pictured over these posters, Satan.

God has been trying to help us. He has always been trying to help us. God has a following of people that are also trying to help. It is a strange world out there. The world is getting worse.

God made and did so many things in His creation that point to a creator, but humans still doubt. Think of all the creatures on this earth. What a variety, and only God could even think of them all. By the way, God created monkeys and apes. When God created man, it was special. He said He made man in His own image and blew the breath of life into us. We did not evolve from an ape. We were created intelligent and could speak a language.

I am going to add a verse that I like about creation from the Bible. I didn't know this verse. We know babies are like a miracle. Well God puts it this way:

Ecclesiastes 11:5

Just as you don't know how the breath of life enters the limbs of a child within its mother's womb you also don't understand how God, who made everything, works.

There are over 7 billion people on this earth that all have different fingerprints. Every one of us have different fingerprints. Only God could do that. Our eyes are all different also since eyes can be scanned by computers and know who is who. God says He knows how many hairs you have on your head. God made it important to be individuals. God wants to meet us individually, and we have to use our free will to go to God, as an individual. Only God can help us and as an individual, we have to ask Him for help. People don't think about the Creator much and ignore Him. Some of course don't believe at all, or don't care. God wants to help those that come to Him.

We humans are impatient, and so if we pray to God, we expect something to happen. God is not human but has all power and knowledge. If you sincerely pray and ask God for help that is what He wants you to do. God already knows you and knows what is best for you. We have an amazing and powerful God, who loves us all, so keep praying. Just don't pray for a new car because you likely won't get it. God is interested in you. He wants you to be interested in Him. He created you, and everything you see. Bad stuff of course is made by men.

God created and set everything up perfectly for life on earth, but man sinned so we are living in it. Do you ever think about what this perfect God gets to see on this earth? You may not believe in God, but if you are wrong, well I don't want to scare anyone. Just think that there is right and wrong, or good and bad on this earth. We can all believe that because we see it. We know about right and wrong from the Bible. God wanted us to understand a lot about right and wrong. Call it sin, or doing wrong is mentioned all through the Bible. Sin is not written about elsewhere, just the Bible. It is a part of this world.

How the planets, and the earth was set up so perfectly for life points to a Creator, God. Many just don't' think of God and take creation and life for granted. We live on a world, and in a country that has some problems. The world and our country will keep getting worse. God's word the Bible tells us it will. Think of our debt or turn the news on for just a few minutes. There is lots of hate and lies. You have to believe what you see and hear. The hate and problems in our world you have to agree is obvious. I don't even enjoy writing about it, but I know God wants me to. It has never, changed, it is called sin. Whether you believe or not, God is not happy with what He sees.

Jesus said the most important thing we humans can do is to love God and to love one another. Sadly, there is not much of that. I'm sure there is still love in families. I pray for everyone out there. God is a loving and merciful God. He is called the Heavenly Father for a reason. He created everything and us.

How long will God put up with the hate, and the wrong that people do to others, and themselves? Only He knows, but He is not just waiting. He is working to save as many as possible. God has a following of people who want to help those that don't believe, or don't care. Think how much God cares. He sent His Son, Jesus to this earth to live as a man, and give up His life for all of us.

Jesus came on a mission from His Father God, to conquer sin, and death as a free gift to man. It was a perfect plan, like the original creation was perfect. Only the Son of God, Jesus could have done this. Jesus gave mankind the way to get back to the Father God. It is amazing what God did for us humans. Jesus gave mankind the way to get back to the Father, God. Jesus came and did what His Father God willed for Him to do. Most people on this earth don't recognize the love of God, and His Son Jesus. That word love is a big word. God and love are one and the same, like God and the Son are one and the same.

Since the wages for sin is death, Jesus died in our place willingly. As He was dying on the cross, He said, Father forgive them for they know not what they do. So Jesus was sacrificed as a free gift for us. We don't think about it enough. What a wonderful and amazing thing. That is the kind of God we have. God raised His Son Jesus from the grave and was very pleased with Him.

So, Jesus is back with His Father God, where He always was before. That makes me think of people asking what was God doing before creation. God has always been living in eternity. Do you think He gets bored? We are human and we can't know some things at least not now. God gave us what He wanted us to know, in the Bible. And by the way, God doesn't get bored and having a Son like Jesus with Him and add the Holy Spirit they have joy together.

It gets interesting this God of ours, and Him having all power we can't really understand that. I think where faith comes in is the Trinity, and I know also being that God is invisible. There are all kinds of proof of God, but

I think of a three in one God might be a little confusing. If this all-powerful God says they are one God it is okay with me.

When God created man the Bible says, let us create man. We start learning more in the Bible about this three in one God. Amazing! You could think of them like a family and they want us to be a part of it. Wow! There are no good enough words for this God, but I do the best I can, and with His help. It is exciting thinking and writing about this God. It is not exciting writing about the sin, and problems we have on the earth. It is not all bad. We have the good creation, love and many good things on this earth. We mainly have God, who made everything man can't make. God made the little seeds, He made flowers for us to see, so many different kinds of animals only He could have thought of them all. Mosquitoes and thorn bushes would have come after sin entered the world.

I know we have a mysterious world, but it would be more of a mystery if God hadn't explained things in the Bible.

Jesus gave us the way, to be with God the Father. Jesus said, " I am the way, the truth, and the life and no man comes to the Father, except through me". A lot was given for us misbehaving humans. God really loves us and wants us to be with Him. When it comes to God no one can understand it all.

I wondered some when writing about God. Let me just say I didn't one day just decide to write about God. No. I wanted God to help the country and the people in the whole world that I know they take creation for granted. Most people don't think about this awesome God. What about all the children, and our schools? We have ape to man and the "big bang". I just ended up somehow writing. I think I had to get permission about the title to the book. I knew I would need help, like how do you write about God, and how He feels about things? I felt like this book would need to be perfect. Well Christians should understand that as a normal American sinner (not bad) I have gotten so much closer to God in doing this book, I'm surprised. I said doing the book because it involved more than writing. Research and more help from God. I say why wouldn't God help me. I am doing this to help people in this troubled world, I didn't think about what it would do for me. This God does work in ways we may not figure on.

We should think about the awesome God we have. We have a God that is called the Trinity. The Bible tells us that we have a three in one God. He has all power, we don't' say they as in three. We don't understand the Trinity or the three in one, being that we are only human. It is interesting. The Bible tells us that God the Father, God the Son and God the Holy Spirit are together as one God. One thing for sure, God can be whatever He wants, do whatever He wants, and be three together, as one God. He lives in eternity, and always has, and always will. The Son of God took off about 2000 years ago and came to this earth. His Father God commanded Him to come to this earth on a mission. God is so interesting being that we hear God is everywhere. I do ask questions about the mystery of God, for myself and for the reader of this. We understand little when it comes to the awesome power of God. Again, I say that is why God gave us the Bible. There are some things He wants us to understand.

Who is the Holy Spirit? What we do know is the Holy Spirit is a great helper. The Holy Spirit was completely behind the writing of the Bible and it being put together. He also miraculously lives in believers to help them to be closer to the Son of God, Jesus.

I've learned things about God I didn't really think about before. Like the Father God has more power than the Son, Jesus. It didn't really matter to me, but I thought it was interesting. Jesus said the Father has more power. The one sending has more power than the one sent. Jesus was sent to this earth over 2000 years ago, by the Father God to save us humans from sin, and death.

After saying all of that, you have to think they are one God. When thinking about the power of God you can imagine anything, and God can do it. In writing this I sometimes get carried away, when thinking of this awesome God. It is OK since I know He wants us to think about Him. Too many don't think about Him. Some think about Him a little. I and most of us have been guilty of not thinking at times of God. I know we have busy lives; we work, take care of our families. We don't think enough about everything you see, including yourself and your family was all created by God. Anything bad, was made by man.

It is interesting, and mysterious living on this world that we know has good things, and bad things. These things are what God wants us to understand. He gave us the Bible to help us to understand. Most people have enough common sense to know bad is bad, and good is good. Like God's original creation, before sin was perfect and good. Well, the whole story to this life really is that this all-powerful God is going to get this world back to the perfect world He first created. That is His will, and He is going to do it. Some humans are going to be with God and help Him and some are not. That is the human story. None of us can be perfect and God fixed that problem for us through His Son Jesus. God does what He needs to do to help us, because He created us and loves us. Some people think that if we have to be perfect like God, we can't have fun. For one thing we can't be perfect. Through Jesus there's a way.

I think just being with God will be fun. Fun is not even a good word for it. To be with the Creator, the one having all power will be, well cool. What words can you say, but cool is ok for how we talk.

People think of this world for fun and whatever. I know it is certainly not all fun for many. This is the only world we know, but none of us can stay here. God has a perfect world in store for us.

God had to give man free will because it was the perfect and right thing to do. Well man sinned and went against God's will. God made a perfect world for men and He loves us. When sin entered the world, well we see today that things are getting worse. Although we still have creation and all the wonders, and beauty from God. Many people are not helping our world with their hate, violence, and many, many more bad things.

Most people have heard about Jesus, and what He did for us. God had to fix the sin problem and He did over 2000 years ago when He willed His Son Jesus to this earth. It is amazing this plan of God's to send His Son. God does perfection like the original creation, and this plan to send His Son Jesus was also perfection and truth. If people really look at this plan, or mission Jesus was sent to do, it is true because it was so perfect. If you study a little about Jesus, He said on this earth that He brings the truth. Jesus was sent by His Father God to do this mission, on this earth, and He made it known that He was doing the will of His Father God. We know that Jesus was also God, God the Son. It is interesting, the one sending has more power than the one sent. When we have God as three in one God (Trinity), I never really thought much about which was more powerful. Jesus himself says the Father has more power. Not that it really matters, but I learned something that is interesting. When you study about God, He is nothing but interesting and wonderful.

Jesus brought the truth to this planet. He was not recognized by man as the Son of God. He did some amazing things and miracles when He was here. This plan of God sending His Son Jesus to die in our place satisfied our debt of sin. The evil in the world or Satan, however you want to look at it were forced to be satisfied that the debt was paid. God did it. No doubt Satan was not pleased, but truth is truth.

I know many people don't believe and many believe differently. Think of those words love and truth. These are two important words God stressed through the Bible.

Is it true that creation just popped up in space, and the planets moved around to set up perfectly? Perfectly for life on planet earth. Is it truth that man evolved from an ape like creature? Is it truth that all life started in soupy pools?

It is springtime, and everything is turning green. Trees are budding out and look at the wildflowers. It is an amazing place, this earth. Look at the sunsets, there is so much beauty. This is what God gave us. If you think of the things that aren't beautiful, we live in a sinful world. That is Satan and our doing. We have so many good things people take for granted. How about the miracle of life itself, and babies we think we know how that happens. Wow! Planting a seed and seeing it grow. There are laws of nature. If you plant a cucumber seed you get cucumber vines, and cucumbers. If you grind wheat and add a few other ingredients and bake it you get a loaf of bread. Even that is like a miracle. Some people think we don't see miracles. This life of ours is a miracle, and miracles are going on all the time. You know we humans have grown accustomed to our world and take everything for granted. We are blessed with all the conveniences for an easier life, so why think of God, the all-powerful Creator of all of it. There is nothing without God.

Life and death are a fact; good and bad is a fact; God and Satan are a fact. All of creation, and life didn't just pop up. After we are all dead and gone from this earth, what would have been the point to it all? Even scientists tell us the sun will burn out in a few billion years or so. We won't need to concern ourselves with that, since we won't last that long. People will destroy themselves, long before the sun gives out.

We have governments around this world that want to be above everyone else. We have people in the world that think they are better than other people. Some because they have more money and some maybe because they think they are smarter. God says He loves us all. He loves us the same. He created us.

Job 34: 19

The One who is righteous and mighty does not grant special favors to princes or prefer important people over the poor people because His hands made them all.

God loves us all, His creation, but doesn't like the sin we do.

People and governments that think they are better than other people and have more power are wrong in their thinking. Only God can make us better, and He does it individually. God doesn't care what color we are, we are all His creation. God wants us to acknowledge Him and love Him back. God wants us to trust Him, and believe also in His Son Jesus, who is the Savior of the world.

We can see everything that God created, and it is amazing. Thanks to God think of the things man has made for us to have an easier life. We can travel and see more creation; we can see it on TV and in pictures. Imagine all of creation; it goes on and on. Think of the creatures we don't see. There is as much by weight of creatures below ground, as all humans above ground. I've heard ants alone weigh close to what humans weigh above ground. So, all creatures below ground weigh more than people above ground. I don't know how they figure it, but it is interesting.

People are the most intelligent creatures on earth. We communicate with one another, we can figure, and make things. We can even figure our life on this earth is temporary. We will all die and leave this world one at a time, or several together. We all miss people, family, and friends that go before us. It hurts and is horrible. There is only one place to understand why such a horrible thing happens to us. The Bible. The Bible tells us about things you can't find out about anywhere else. Maybe you've heard God the Holy Spirit was an influence on the Bible. Why do you think God wanted us to have His Word, the Bible? We know most people on this earth don't believe in the Bible, God or creation. Many do.

The Bible has information you can't get anywhere else. It gives us a history of the beginning of our time. The Bible is an amazing book. Some of it you can just read and some of it requires a little study. Some people will say it was written by man. That is true, but a little study and it points to God's influence. There is a lot to it. It is a history of the world. Not God's world, but our world. God lives outside of time, and in eternity. You don't have to believe in the Bible, and whether you believe, or not is also talked about in the Bible. Is the Bible God's Word? Of course! I read about a scientist that wanted to prove the Bible wrong, so he tried to find it fallible. He ended up becoming a christian. There are many things in the Bible that are harder to understand than other things. It was written by different writers, but certainly has God's influence. The words God says in the Bible is way beyond, what people can say. So many prophecies in the Bible that have come true and many that we all wait for. God doesn't just see the future; He also makes it happen. There is nothing out there like the Bible. God loves us, His creation, and that's why He gave us the Bible. With creation already here, man needed more to believing in an invisible God. The Bible tells us of a time when there was no Bible. There was a greater presence of God back then. He gave the Hebrew (Jewish) people the Ten Commandments. You have to read the Bible to understand. Now that we have the Bible we can believe in God, or not. God gave us free will, the Bible tells us this. If you figure the over 7 billion people on this earth, that all have different fingerprints, most of them don't believe in God, or the Bible. Creation, and the Bible, people still are not believing; what more can God do? It is interesting, and most of it is a mystery. Whether you believe or not, life is a great mystery. We all can believe that is true.

Think about what God did for us. He made it very plain in His Word, the Bible. He made sure over and over again that He sent His Son, Jesus to die in our place because of our sins. He raised His Son from death back to life and we can follow. God did it that way because it had to be that way. Man sinned and we can't be with a sinless and holy God as a sinner. God sent His Son Jesus on a mission. In short Jesus came to give man a way to come back to the Father God, sinless. It was a perfect plan. You would have to say that Satan and the bad in the world would have to agree that this sacrifice was acceptable. God the Son gave up His life willingly for all of us.

Let's think of this mission Jesus was sent to accomplish. Jesus was tempted by Satan and didn't sin. He told Satan to leave Him, and He only did His Father's will. Since God said to man the wages for sin is death. So eventually Jesus paid for our sins. He was spit on, criticized, beat on, whipped half to death, and then crucified and died. He did this of His own free will, and His Father God willed Him to do this. So, God the Son gave up His life for us not deserving it. He took our sins with Him when He died. He also defeated death; His Father God raised Him back to life. The mission God sent His Son Jesus to do was finished. God the Father was very pleased with Jesus His Son. So now through what Jesus did for us, we have a way to be with God. The Bible calls this a free gift. That is the love of God.

If you check out the Bible, it was predicted many times of Jesus' coming up to thousands of years before He came to this earth. It tells about some of what Jesus would do while here. When Jesus was here, He fulfilled these prophecies. It is easy to check where prophecies are in the Bible, with the internet. Just have a Bible close to look at them. There are hundreds of prophecies in the Bible, and God makes sure they come true. These prophecies are proof of God. Thinking about proof of God is not just something I say, but God gives us that. He gave us creation and the Bible, and all the prophecies in the Bible. Only God can predict future events, or make things happen. I would also say, He made humans. Common sense has to tell us that humans are special on this planet, and something more special made us. God says we are special. He says He created us in His image, and He loves us.

Why do scientists and professor types of people compare humans to other creatures on this earth? Well, they couldn't compare us to snakes, rabbits or any other animal. Oh, so we are closest to looking like a monkey or an ape. This is just Satan at work, wanting us to not consider God at all. God created all kinds of monkeys and apes. He didn't make them special like He did us. Everything created is for us.

We have two choices of what we can believe. Of course, people can believe in nothing and many do. Those people can believe in the mystery of life, and just live their life out on this earth. We can trust and believe in God, or believe in what atheists, scientists, and professors tell us. They tell us of the "Big Bang" in empty space, soupy pools where life originated, and ape to man. Shame on them because that seems to stick. It is taught to our children, and it is in our natural science museums. It is just cold thinking.

God says He created man in His image, and we didn't evolve; we were perfect and had a language. We could talk to God. God talks about love. He loves us, and wants us to love Him back, and He wants us to love one another. God of course gave us a choice, so we don't have to love Him back. It is interesting to me. Does love win in the end or does hate?

God is in charge and wants things to be perfect the way original creation was before sin.

It took some doing, and is taking some doing, but God is going to make things perfect again. He wants to bring as many that will join Him. Many on this planet love God and more don't think about all of it. Love is stronger than hate and will win out in the end. Love is the most important word in our language. You could say God is, but God is love, and Love is God.

Jesus when He came to this planet, mentioned love. He said the greatest commandment was to love God, then to love one another. It would make for a more perfect world. Think of what God the Father sent God the Son, Jesus to do on this planet for us. That is love.

Think of the cold, and lack of love some scientists and professors, tell us about creation. It also doesn't make sense and it is their theory. They even say they are not sure. How can you be sure? These kind of educated people work with theories. On the other hand, God tells us the facts. He tells the truth. There are so many things in creation that point to God.

We just take these things for granted. Everyone is born into this creation. Creation before sin entered on this planet is still here. Look at the sunsets, the wildflowers and so much beauty. Think of what man can't make.

A seed you plant it, and it grows what plant it came from, no change. Animals mate with the same animals. These are part of the laws of nature. God's laws, and only He could do this. We have bad things in our world and only the Bible explains about it. Satan and humans cause the sin in this world. That is why we have the beauty from God, and the ugliness from sin. God just keeps on giving; like He gave us creation and He gave us the Bible. He has a following of people that try to help Him. They are called the children of God. God wants to add to this following.

Some people are loving, some are cold, and some are just filled with hate. People can be every way in between these. God can only be one way, although He can have a temper like us, when it comes to sin. God is truth, loving, and merciful. Only God can help us to be this way.

We have such an influence of God in our world, and the Bible. Some countries don't allow God's Word, the Bible in their country, mostly communist countries. They want their people to put the state first, not God. They don't believe in God. Some countries don't believe in the true God. God says there is only one God. Some religions say Christians believe in three Gods. They can take that up with God, who has all power. God the Father, God the Son, and God the Holy Spirit are together as one God. The Bible talks a lot about this awesome God. If He says He is three in one I'm not going to argue. There is no way for us to understand this all-powerful God. He gave us the Bible to help us understand a lot.

There are many religions around the world, and our country. It seems that being human you think of the religion you are in is the best. Religions are a manmade thing to worship God, but religions are not mentioned in the Bible. To worship God is a good thing, but to have a personal relationship with God, is what God wants. Not to say that God shouldn't be worshipped, because He should. I'm just saying God helps us one on one. It is also interesting that He can help millions all at the same time. I hope and pray that happens.

All religions should go by the one Bible, but they don't. We are humans and humans think differently. There is one God, and He doesn't change, and His Word the Bible doesn't change.

Another thing, we have besides creation, and the Bible is Israel. Why has this tiny country been focused on since the beginning of time? They are God's chosen people. Were they better than other people? No! There weren't a lot of people on the planet back then.

God intended for the Hebrews (Jews) to help people in the world to know God. He wanted them to be priests, prophets and be close to Him. Like all humans it didn't work out well. Back in those days there was a lot of idol worship around. Egypt and countries worshipped lots of different Gods. Israel back then didn't have the Bible, but they had God closer in their lives. They had the Ten Commandments. Things went well when they did God's will. God would warn them through prophets usually if they were doing wrong. God blessed them when they did right and when they did wrong, He would punish them.

God's chosen people are talked about a lot in the Bible. They have had good and bad happen to them since early times, and more recent times. If you didn't believe in God, or the Bible then the Jews are a problem. You have to believe in the Jews because they are here, and in Israel. Christians focus on the tiny little country. Why? Anything that happens there could be interesting, because of God and His chosen people. The Bible predicted, or God did that Israel would become a new state. The Jews were dispersed throughout the world long ago. Some unlucky ones ended up in Russia, Germany, Poland and other places. History tells us what happened to them. Millions of them were slaughtered by Hitler during World War II. The Jews were prominently wealthy people. They were into banking, jewelry sales, and different money-making businesses. It is that way with the Jews in America. They got into motion pictures and other things that make them money. The Jews have had it rough though, through much of their history. They have also been blessed. Well, the blessing continues because they are God's chosen people . God does not change. I will write a few prophecies from the Bible about God's chosen people, the Jews. These are just more predictions by God that have come true.

Amos 9:14-15 written about 750 B.C.

I will restore my people Israel. They will rebuild the ruined cities and live in them. They will plant vineyards and drink the wine from them. They will plant gardens and eat their fruit. I will plant the people of Israel in their land and they won't be uprooted again from the land I gave them, says the Lord your God.

Ezequiel 34:13 written between 593 and 571 BC

I will bring them out of the nations, gather them from the countries, and bring them to their own land. I will take care of them on the mountains of Israel, by the streams, and in the inhabited places of land.

Jeremiah 31;10 written 626 to 586 B.C.

Hear the word of the Lord. You nations listen to the word of the Lord. Tell it to the distant islands. Say, the one who scattered the people of Israel will gather them and watch over them as a shepherd watches over His flock. The Lord will free the descendants of Jacob and reclaim them from those who are stronger than they are.

Leviticus 26: 11-12

I will put my tent among you, and I will never look at you with disgust. So, I will live among you and be your God, and you will be my people.

These are very interesting prophecies from the Bible, and there are many more. You should look at the prophecies in the Bible, they are proof of God. Israel is doing well, and with God watching over them they will do well. We live in an imperfect world so Israel still will have problems, like we all do. You get the idea why Christians and others watch this tiny country, Israel.

Do you think of what we have that gives us an easier life? Most of us know how Americans washed clothes in the old days. Think back to that day and time. Life was harder. Now we have washers, dryers, dishwashers, microwaves, and you know the list goes on. We have our transportation, air travel, computers, cell phones and IPads. Yes, this country was blessed. It was blessed because we originally put God first. One nation under God and in God we trust. That means something to us, and it means something to God. Things started changing with atheists pushing God out of our schools. We know some companies wanted to say Happy Holidays instead of Merry Christmas. How is our country doing today? Are things getting worse? I know we can't ever pay the trillions of dollar debt we owe. There is so much hate in our government; they don't work for the people anymore. Most of them care only about the vote, and power. Shame on them. I'm sure there are a few that want to do what is right. Some in our government stay there so long that they lose touch with real people. They become more interested in making the people feel like them. I mean doing what they want us to do. Like they know best. I see these government people like little children. Excuse me little children for comparing you to them.

I mean they throw tantrums and say awful things if they don't get their way. It pours outside the government also. There is a following of people that say bad things or do bad things to other people that don't totally agree with their philosophy of life, the way they think it should be. Shame.

Another thing God didn't go anywhere, He is watching. The rest of the world is mostly worse off than America. At least we have some freedom.

God is not pleased with the condition of the world, or what is happening in America. We have, or mostly have everything for a good life. We got these things from this earth. We got metals, glass, fuels and much more. We made things to make life better.

All through time peoples lives had to get worse before we called to God for help. Humans have always since the beginning of time gotten closer or further away from God. Most of us have at one time or another. Of course, some never get close to God, and I should say a lot. We have problems in this world of ours, and God wants to help us. Again, I'll say you have to use your free will God gave you and seek Him. God is invisible so how do you seek Him? God is everywhere, and He wants you to acknowledge Him. What should you say to God? Being that you are talking to a perfect and holy God you should say you are sorry. God hates sin, but He loves you. Since everyone on this planet sins in some way, we are all guilty. Tell God you love Him also. He has always loved you. Always.

God is everyone's heavenly Father, the Creator of us, and everything. He wants to have a relationship with you. Not just once or twice a year or an hour on Sunday, but all the time. Check out the Bible, which is and always will be God's Word. He did something for you and everyone over 2000 years ago when He sent His Son to die in our place because of our sin. God raised His Son Jesus back to life.

I've said before we live in a mysterious world. It is also interesting. It is a mystery that God wanted to create man at all, since He knew we would be trouble. Did God want more company through eternity? Maybe, who knows? We do know that the smartest people on this planet have the same mystery we all have. So, they guess about creation. Most of those educated people don't bring God into creation. There are atheists that believe in their studies. Things like life and creation were set up too perfectly to be able to explain it. So much life and varieties that it points to a Creator, God. Why don't people acknowledge this Creator, God? Maybe because we can't see Him, like the wind. Maybe because we don't have to acknowledge Him or believe in Him. God himself made sure we had that right, or free will to acknowledge Him, or not. It gets back to that big word, love. God and His Word, the Bible, talks about this word and His Son Jesus talked about love when He was on planet earth. Why is God (the Trinity) so focused on us humans? There is no way that we humans, the over 7 billion of us on this planet, with different fingerprints just happened somehow. We certainly didn't evolve from an ape. All life didn't come from soupy pools.

The problem with people is we doubt and take everything for granted. The answers to life are there in front of us. It is so amazing, and point straight to God, that has all power. We go back to what God gave us, free will. You don't have to believe, and we take life for granted.

Why did God give us wildflowers? He loves us and He wanted to. I think God gave us such an abundance of life on the planet; it would be a little tough ruling out the Creator, God. God keeps giving; He gave His Son Jesus, who is the Savior of the world. Creation was perfect and the mission of Jesus was perfect. Well, we do have plenty of non-perfect on this planet. That is Satan and our fault for sin. God set a high standard for people, perfection, so He had to fix the sin problem. Only God could fix it for all people so God the Son, Jesus came and fixed it. Is it all too much to believe in, for most people? God gave us so much proof of himself, but most people will just live their lives out on this earth, and not think about it. God is working and has a following of people trying to help. God is not giving up on you.

We humans seem to always need reminders or more, and more education about God. I did and we all do. We all live on this earth with the bad and good. None of us is perfect. We all need to get close to God. I'm reminding you that this universe didn't spring up from a "big bang" in empty space billions and billions of years ago. Ancient life did not come from comets, and soupy pools. Man did not evolve from ape. Shame on these educated people that push these unknown ideas. That is pretty much what our children are taught in our schools. Our schools where God is not very welcome. Scientists that don't believe in God, are responsible for posters in science museums depicting ape to man.

Believe or not the worst thing on this planet is Satan. He wants all of our children, and all of us to not believe in God. This battle you can call it between God and Satan (or sin) has been going on since the creation of man. Humans are caught in the middle between God and Satan. We don't understand all of this for sure, but we do know there is good and bad in the world. Anyone paying attention knows it is getting worse. All you have to do is turn on the news. How about many of the awful commercials on TV? There is more division and just pure hate in the world, and lots of lying.

This writing is another reminder that God does not change, and He still loves us like He always has. God is the same as always, and He doesn't want us falling for Satan, or the bad in the world, but to come to Him. He wants to help and only He can. I don't think you would fall for Satan, but if you don't choose God you automatically get Satan. Sorry for being so blunt, but it is the truth. You can reach God through Jesus the Son.

It appears that the world leans to believing scientists, and professors about creation. I know you can go to a natural science museum, where they have skeletons of dinosaurs. These dinosaur bones are facts, and enjoyable to look at. These museums also have large posters depicting ancient man. The museum I went to did. There were like 5 or 6 stooped over hairy ape creatures and the last one stood straight. He was a man. There were dates below each creature. I should say there should have been a seventh creature shown above the rest depicting the one responsible for the poster, Satan. He doesn't want you to believe, or even think about God.

Scientist ideas on creation and the universe are just ideas. They don't know for sure and they will tell you that. There is no way to know for sure. One more place to hear about creation is the Bible. You don't have to believe in the Bible, but it sure makes sense. The Bible says God was the Creator of everything. God says in the Bible, He created man and woman perfectly, and they were intelligent. They had a language. They talked to God. God gave us a Bible. If He only gave us creation, we would wonder where everything came from.

There are so many things in creation that point to a Creator, God. In writing this book I needed to check many things I didn't know or didn't think of. We know our sun is a perfect distance away for life to be possible. In the universe there are lots of stars, and lots of suns. There are very few suns like ours, from what we are capable of knowing. Our sun is also the perfect size sun for life on this planet. Scientists say there are dwarf suns out there, that could have sustained life on planets around it. There is a problem with these small suns. They are very active and aggressive with solar flares so planets even at the right distance get scorched. I didn't know much about different sized suns and what difference they are compared to our sun. Scientists like to look for places life could possibly exist. I'm finding out many things about how our solar system was set up so perfectly. Some suns and the universe are more violent than others, but our sun is the right size and not so violent. It is also the perfect distance, from us. Suns and our sun shoot out solar rays and worse gamma rays, and particles. These rays are radiation and are harmful and can kill you. The earth has a magnetic field around it protecting us from these harmful particles. I'm not going to try to explain this, magnetic field, but you can check it out. Earth also has an atmosphere that protects us. I write about our sun, magnetic fields, and our atmosphere, because it all needed to be set up this way for life to exist on earth.

People should think of creation and how it was set up. Some scientists have loosened up a little and call it creative design. I guess most of them don't want to say God. Some people want to give space aliens part or all credit for human DNA and maybe creation. I know leaving God out, is exactly what Satan wants. Also you would have to wonder who created space aliens. The more you think of creation, the perfect set up for life, the Bible, all prophecies in the Bible, you have to go out of your way to think of alternatives to a powerful Creator. The more I learn about a perfect creation, the Bible and all; it is not explainable without God. Only God could set everything for life on earth. God sure put I huge variety of life on this earth. I believe God puts things into creation that makes us wonder. We certainly can't know an all-powerful God, just think about the strange creatures on earth, and in our oceans. He doesn't even have to think about making these animals. God just wills it, and it happens. We certainly have trouble grasping that.

How about the over 7 billion people on earth that have different fingerprints? We know how the law uses fingerprints. The tiny ends of our fingers and how could they all be different. We also have different eyes. These things are amazing and point to God. All the marvels that we see point to God. We know most people just live their life as best they can but take God's creation for granted.

I'm sure most of us have heard loud thunder but think of the thunder we don't hear so often. The thunder that cracks so loud it makes us jump a little. I think we should think of that as God trying to get our attention. It takes that kind of crash to stir us. We mostly continue to do what the earth has to offer us, and don't think what God has to offer us. There are many believers out there, but none of us is as close to God as He wants us to be. We all live on this good and bad world that looks to be getting worse. The Bible says it is going to get worse. God is going to do His will, and eventually make things perfect again. People don't look for the evidence of God. We can't see God so why look? Well, we have a mystery because the evidence of God is everywhere. It seems like the evidence of God everywhere is being kept quiet on this planet. We know everything was set up perfectly on this planet for life and all the varieties of life. With all the proof of God we have to realize there is a problem. That is Satan and sin. Satan wants you not to believe or consider God. Why? God loves us and Satan hates God. I'm sure many don't believe in Satan, or God. Well, you can believe in the good and bad on this planet, that doesn't appear to get better.

No one has the answer to life, and the good and bad and the mystery to all of it. God does and that is why He continually wants to help. We have to want His help. Understand, or not it was set up with humans, and God like creation and everything else. God gave humans free will and He wants us to use that free will and go to Him.

God has a plan for every individual on this planet. A lot of humans will never find out about the plan God has for your life, because you don't even pay attention, or recognize God. God wants an individual relationship with you. You don't even have to go to church to have this individual relationship with God. The thing is you can learn more about God through a good church. You can be around other believers that want to worship this all-powerful God.

God created everything and all of us, and to think of having an individual relationship with God, who has all power and knowledge is a wonderful thing. I would say the experience with God is subtle and relaxed, not like a human relationship. God is invisible and you likely will only hear Him in your mind. Some might say to believers our God is invisible and doesn't talk to us so there is no God. I would say to nonbelievers, first God is not human. Then all the beauty on this planet point straight to God. Also, we don't see the wind, but it is there. Believers pray for non-believers and the Bible tells us that we all will face God eventually.

If you were to think of creation, and how it was all set up for life on this planet, you might be surprised. If you were to take one small plant, and learn about it, you would be surprised. The inner workings of that plant and what it does. It takes in carbon dioxide and gives off oxygen. If it was the only little plant on this earth it would be like a miracle. Now think of millions of plants on the earth. So many varieties of plant life, and then think of the creatures on this earth. So many varieties of life on earth and in our oceans. Some creatures and ocean life are strange to us. You would have to think only God could think of such creatures. Most people I'm afraid don't think about where plants, creatures, us, and the universe came from. It is a whole lot of stuff to think it just happened. Scientists can't explain it, and, how could they? They gave us their ideas leaving God out. They tell us about a "big bang" in empty space, the soupy pools, where life supposedly started and ape to man. Well, shame on them. It hurts our children especially, and all people. It takes their mind off of God. Whether you believe or not Satan is busy trying to keep our mind off of God. With God's help I'm trying to put peoples mind back on God. None of this would matter except God says it does matter. If we just all eventually died, and that was all, it all wouldn't matter, but that is not the way it will be. I think our common sense should tell us, what would be the point to all of this if eventually we are all dead and gone.

We all have to live on this earth and only God can help. God got all of this started, with creation and us. He gave us free will; we sinned and actually messed things up.

You should figure that this all-powerful God is going to fix things and bring everything back to perfection. That is just the way He is. He wants as many that will, to join Him.

God has helped us by giving us the Bible. God wanted to let us know certain things. Why wouldn't He since we are His creation, and He loves us. Let's see we have creation that didn't just happen, we have the Bible, but it is still not enough to make people believe. Most people just don't think about it much at all. How can people ignore all the prophecies in the Bible? No one can predict the future or cause future events to happen. God does, and hundreds of things have happened that God said that would happen. They are going to keep happening.

Many of us wonder what is going on, on this earth. It is getting worse in many ways. We see the protests on the streets, and the destruction and violence. There should be stand-ups for God or get togethers on our street. Of course, the world, and a lot of people wouldn't like that.

People think we have to be good boys and girls to be close to God. We all fail there since we are all sinners. Actually, you can't be good boys and girls without God. We all live on this good and bad world. Christians and non-Christians all sin. We are not perfect even us believers. There is a difference between Christians and non-Christians. Christians realize the world has problems, and they have problems, so they went to God seeking help. God is perfect and is there with free help. God gave people help through His Son, Jesus who is Savior of all who believe. So, when we believe we become sinless? Yes and no. We have been forgiven by God through His Son, Jesus, God the Son. With that kind of gift, we want to do what is right. Living in this world we fail sometimes, but we can ask God for forgiveness. Don't think you can't go to God or get close to Him. because you do things that are wrong. Only He can help, as long as you really want help. It is just the way it is that we have to choose God. Humans should seek the Creator. He gave us that freedom, or free will and He wants us to use it and seek Him. God is the reason we live and walk on this planet. He also gave us the right to do our will not His. He gave us that right. There is a big problem if we ignore the Creator, and don't seek this all-powerful God. Well, we lose. We have to want God in our life by our own free will. We all get to choose, and God gave us that choice. God loves you and wants you to choose Him. God is working and many people are working with God to help save as many people as possible. It is simple as that, and time will eventually run out. God doesn't want to lose anyone. I believe we will know when time gets shorter, by this world.

I am writing while something else has happened in our world. A pestilence called corona virus. I won't start telling you we are in the end times, but things are getting worse. When I started this book, I think we were around 25 trillion dollars in debt, and we won't come back from that. The hate and division in our country, and our government tells us a lot. I, of course don't even like writing about the problems, but I have to write the facts. I do pray for everyone out there. I think the rest of the world is even worse off than us. I like to be optimistic, but I can see.

I'm sure we will eventually get by the corona virus and what then? Who knows with us humans, and the sin in the world? Corona virus, tornadoes, hurricanes just seem to spawn in a sinful world. It was set in motion way back with Adam and Eve. I believe when we leave God to the side things get worse. Many are not leaving God to the side, but we still live on this earth. We all just need to pray. We should all try not to be afraid, because God is in charge, and is where He always has been. Everywhere. God is watching and waiting and working.

This country or I should say our government tried to be fair in our schools years ago when it came to people that didn't believe in God. One lady I recall used the word equality and pretty much removed God from our schools. Of course, you can't change God, but the people can ignore God. When we built this nation, we made it 1 nation under God, and in God we trust. I believe America thrived, and became as powerful as we are today, because we put God first. Instead of hate and division our government and others need to get back to 1 nation under God, and in God we trust. Many in our government care about their power. What is power? God has power. Most Americans are smart people, and we don't care about your power. The people are still waiting for you, the government to work for us and help the country. We've waited so long now; our government with their hunger for power may have ruined us.

People today seem to be in a hurry doing everything. We are like busy bees going this way and that. Talking or texting on our phones. It is easy to get caught up doing worldly things. We are humans, and sometimes get involved in things, and some things that are not good. People can be busy and tied up with their iPads and they don't have time for God. There are so many things we can think of, instead of this invisible God. Most things we can do on this planet are good things. God gave us many things to do, just because of creation.

God wanted to let men understand certain things, so He gave us the Bible. The Bible is a wonder in itself. The Bible has been around for a long time. No one has proved it wrong. All prophecies today in the Bible have come true. We might not understand all that is in the Bible, but we also can't understand this all-powerful, all-knowing God.

If we think of creation, the Bible says God created man in His own image. The creation of man is the first time the Bible says let us make man, Plural. You can't make this stuff up. God lets us know many times that He is one God, with His Son Jesus, and the Holy Spirit. This God of ours is amazing. We might not understand at all, but we can't understand God having all power, and knowledge. The Bible is full of things you can't make up because they are true from God. So many prophecies and only God knows the future, and also makes future things happen. The things that are of more importance are all through the Bible. God wanted us to know of His Son, Jesus. There were prophecies all through the Old Testament about Jesus' coming. It tells about some things Jesus will do when He comes.

Back to Adam and Eve, God told them they could eat from any tree in that garden, but not from the one in the middle of the garden. He warned them that if they did, they would surely die. There were lots of fruit trees and bushes of great things to eat in that garden, but only one tree God said not to eat from. Any of us would have done the same after being tempted by Satan. I know we have a mystery here, but life is a mystery. We don't understand why God permitted Satan to tempt Eve. God knew what would happen, man was going to sin. Since God gave us that freedom, or free will He wanted to see who would seek His help, of their own free will. That has really been the story since time began, is who is going to seek a relationship with God. God wants an individual relationship with us. He created us to be individuals, like all of us having different fingerprints, different eyes. He knows each individual on earth, and even how many hairs on your head.

We can't understand a lot of this, especially the battle between Satan and God. Satan is an angel, not like us, but was given free will like us. We have a way to be with God through His Son, Jesus. Satan does not, he was with God, but still rebelled. Satan was created a powerful angel but wanted more power like God. Satan was kicked out of heaven to this earth. That is another mystery since we didn't need Satan. We can do wrong without Satan's help.

If you look at our world, we should know why God gave us the Bible, His Word. God mainly wanted to tell us we needed to come to Him.

There are many mysteries in our world. Thinking of God, if we didn't have God, the Bible, or anything we would have a bigger mystery, or one we could never explain at all. The thing is we do have a Creator that loves us. His creation. He created us in His image.

We don't care for some people; well God created them and loves us all. God just says He doesn't like the sin, we do. God had to fix that, and He did through what His Son came and did 2000 years ago.

Thinking of people and God and that is what this book is about, people and God. You can see many people out in the world, even on TV or sitting in a parking lot at a store, you can watch people moving around. I say this because people are above all the rest of creation. People can figure they can make plans, and they can make things happen. People are intelligent. I know you might argue that point, but you know what I'm saying. Basically, people are amazing. I've used that word, amazing in this book a lot talking about God. If people are amazing, we need a new vocabulary in talking about God. Like God says He created us in His own image, and we are special and amazing. We should then think of God and how special and amazing He is. For one thing He is the great Father God, because He created us. Many people don't think of this invisible God at all, or very seldom. God is not human like us, and He is everlasting. God breathes into every human and gives us life and we have a spirit. We have a body that wears out or gets old. Why doesn't the spirit inside us get old? Most people don't think about that, but it's true. The Bible says when we die our spirit will not die. We are all a part of God, actually everything is, but we are special. We certainly didn't evolve from an ape-like creature. Man was never an animal; God created man completely separate from the animals. Now of course jokingly we can say there are animals out there that are human. It is the sin in the world that we have people that are like animals. I should apologize to the animals since they only do what they do. People have a choice.

If you could think in God's place after creating man, you would give men freedom or free will to think how he wanted. You would not want robot types of people that had to love you. You would want them to know of you and love you by their own free will. It was this free will, although it was right that God gave it to us, but it caused all the world problems. Man sinned or went against God's wishes. So, we see the world of today. Like I said before God is perfect and He created perfect and He is going to make things perfect again. Since we can't be with a perfect God as sinners, God had to fix things. How do you fix this sin problem between God and man? God knows all, and He knew what had to be done. For some reason God wants us to be with Him for eternity. God had the perfect plan, and most people know the story of Jesus. Do you think much about this plan? It is really amazing. It was a simple and perfect plan, but also showed God's love for us. Jesus, God's Son was sent into this world on a mission to take care of His Father's plan. Jesus was to grow up like a human and go through everything we do. Jesus was tempted to do wrong like we are but didn't sin. He was here to do His Father's will. The Bible predicted Jesus, called the Messiah, long before He ever came. Leaders of the religious order back then expected Jesus to come with great power and to fix everything.

The Jewish people during the time of Jesus were under Roman rule. The Jewish people knew their scrolls, or part of the early Bible, said the Messiah, Jesus was coming. Jesus was prophesized to come. They figured Jesus would fix all their problems. When Jesus did come it was not like what they thought, so the leaders at that time didn't recognize Him. Jesus did so many miracles while He was on this earth. Jesus came as more of a teacher of His Father God, to love God, and to love one another. The Jewish religious leaders back then didn't like hearing that Jesus was the Messiah, the Son of God. With the Romans in control the Jewish religious leaders were concerned and disturbed by the following Jesus was getting. They wanted and felt they needed to put a stop to it. So, we know the story they got the Romans to crucify Jesus. The big picture to this was Jesus came and did exactly what His Father God willed for Him to do. Jesus willingly laid down His life for humans by taking on the sin Himself, our sin, and dying in our place. He was innocent and He was God the Son. It was a perfect plan. His Father God was certainly pleased with His Son.

Jesus did what was prophesized. The Jewish religious leaders failed to understand Jesus didn't come just for them, but to save the world. God raised Jesus to life again, and what Jesus did here on this planet is what God the Father willed Him to do. The Jewish religious leaders back then, and people today think what they want. It was enough that Jesus gave His life for all of us. Jesus also was on this earth to push love and peace, not to kill Romans.

So, we had a perfect creation by God, and after sin God fixed it with a perfect plan. God gave us all these things, and the Bible to tell us about it all.

Many of us have questions that won't get answered from the Bible. I know God wants us to learn. We learn by having an open mind. Some people in this world don't want others to have an open mind. They want us to think and believe like they do. God wants us to have the freedom of thought, and to investigate life. We should seek the truth because it is the right thing to do. You may run into those who think Christians are brainwashed by their families, to believe in God. It really doesn't matter, because we still have to investigate and learn, each of us.

You have to look at this world, and how everything was set up for life. All the varieties of life on this planet. Science will tell us it just happened, or it just popped up possibly, not sure, and maybe. Why do they jump around telling us about how creation and life happened, but won't use one word, God? Thinking of the earth with the good and the bad, it sounds like battle. Which side is winning? Since we all will eventually die, do we want to be remembered for doing good or bad? If what many people think that when you are dead, you are dead and gone, and that's it. It wouldn't matter if you were good or bad. Is this good and bad in the world like a test? Are there too many questions and not enough answers? Look and think about us humans, we want truthful answers. We are impatient, we want to be satisfied, and the world is not giving us any of this. We have something interesting and mysterious, and many of us feel the presence of God. There is a lot about creation we don't understand so how can we understand God that has all power and knowledge? We humans living in this good and bad world, just doubt and doubt. Not all people doubt.

God says He is the heavenly Father, the Creator but we just doubt. The magnificent way creation and life was set up, we still doubt, but not all of us. God gave us more to help us understand, the Bible. I'm sure God shakes His head and grimaces a little because most humans still doubt. How much more does God need to give us, so we quit doubting? It is not enough that everything beautiful on this earth point to God. Many doubt and many don't seem to care. There is something out there, and everywhere that has always been there.

He is trying to get your attention. He is perfect and has all power. He is God. An example of God is your soul or spirit inside you. As we get older and get aches and pains, do we feel the same inside? Yes. Some people might feel a little bitter or unhappy they can't do what they want to do anymore. Only the body wears out not the spirit. Call it the breath of life God breathed into us. We can only thank God for creating us humans. We have more questions than answers. There are people that have hard lives because they have problems physically, just another mystery on a good and bad world. These people that hurt are not being punished by God. It is just the world we live on, which is an imperfect world. God has always wanted perfection, happiness, love, and all the good things. That is the way God is. Since God is all-powerful and can do anything people have always wanted Him to fix things in their lives. Think what Jesus said, Father it is not what I will, but what You will.

Since we are born with creation already here, and the Bible, we humans mostly just take it all for granted. This earth and the rest of the universe were either created, or it just happened somehow. The Bible says God created everything and humans. God gave us the Bible because He loves us, His creation, and He wants us to know about certain things.

There are many things that point to God, that are not in the Bible. Like fingerprints. Over seven billion people on this planet have different fingerprints. That seems impossible. God made us to be individuals. His Word says He knows how many hairs you have on your head.

There are so many things in creation that point to God. He gave us such an abundance in creation that there would be no doubt, it had to be created by a Supreme Being, God. People still doubt, it is just the way we are. God gave us freedom, or free will. It was the right thing for Him to do. So, you can believe or not.

God had to give us His Word, the Bible, to let us know about creation and why there is life and death. He wanted us to know that He did not create us to die. He says in His Word, that this death problem, He fixed through His Son Jesus. God loves us and has done so many things for us. Is it ever going to be enough for most humans to even acknowledge God?

Do you think about God much? We know the answer, some yes, some no, and all kinds in between. Do you think about why God thinks about you all the time? You are His creation, and He loves you, it is that simple. He doesn't like what some of us do, and that is what gets more complicated.

Most children on this earth have mothers and fathers that love them and want the best for them. God is greater and loves us all and wants the best for all of us. He has always tried to let us know, He is the Creator, and our Heavenly Father. He wants us to know that only He can help us. We certainly don't understand a lot about this earth, and the universe.

God already fixed our problems when He sent His Son Jesus to this earth to save us from sin. Most people know the story of Jesus. Some people believe, and some may think it is just a story. Whether you believe or not you should think of this plan of God's. It came from God and was a perfect plan. Jesus was to come and live and become a man as we do. He was tempted but never sinned. Jesus was here on a mission, and that mission was to do His Heavenly Father's will. If you think of Jesus, you are thinking of God. Since our God is a three in one God (Trinity) God the Father, God the Son, and God the Holy Spirit. They have always been together as one God.

We celebrate Jesus at Christmas and Easter. I've written about this earth we live on with the good and the bad. Why is the birth of Jesus discounted by Santa Claus, and the Easter Bunny, and hunting Easter eggs? I'm not saying that those things are bad, but what Jesus did can't be compared.

Just like creation was perfect, the plan of what Jesus did for us humans was perfect. Again, being that we are all sinners on this planet, that had to be fixed. God fixed it through His Son Jesus. Only God could fix a sin problem in this world, so God the Son was sent to do it. Remember that God the Father, and God the Son and God the Holy Spirit had joy being together and love each other. They work together as one God and are one God.

Jesus did many miracles while He was on this earth. The main thing was taking the sin of the world on Himself and giving up His life freely for us. His Father God wanted Him to do this. Jesus did give humanity a way to be with the Father God again without sin. We now only have to believe Jesus took away our sins. Can we believe that Jesus did this? Can we believe this story? Satan and this world don't want us to believe. The thing is there's a lot of proof of Jesus. Even though Jesus' time was 2000 years ago, nothing from the past jumps out to say it is not true. No! Too many people knew Jesus or knew of

Him in those days. Even after being raised back to life, from His Father God many saw Him.

There are hundreds of prophecies in the Bible about Jesus' coming, like hundreds to a thousand or more years before He came. Why so many predictions of Jesus? The Bible is for humans, and Jesus came and died for us so we could have that chance to live forever. Do people want to live forever? God has all wisdom, and originally created the Garden of Eden, a perfect utopian, sinless world. It will be more enjoyable than we can imagine.

We have an easier way of looking for prophecies or versus in the Bible. Get online and have a Bible to check it out. Again, there are hundreds of prophecies of Jesus' coming, and some saying what will happen.

For instance, Isaiah 7:14 therefore the Lord himself shall give you a sign: behold a Virgin shall conceive, and bear a son, and shall call His name Immanuel.

We don't know a lot about Jesus 'younger life, probably since He didn't begin His mission until He was around 30.

We do know Jesus helped His earthly father. They were carpenters. They made things with wood. I bet Jesus and His earthly father got small wounds occasionally, in that kind of work. I kind of bet Jesus took care of those. We know He did one other miracle, when there was a wedding reception in Cana. Halfway through the get together they were running out of wine. Jesus' mother, Mary, told Jesus because she knew He could do something. Jesus told her it wasn't time for Him to start this sort of thing. Miracles. His mother told some other help to do what Jesus told them to do. He told them to fill up six large urns with water. When it was dipped out it was wine. It was commented on at the party that usually people drank the best wine first and save lesser wine for later. The wine in the urns was the best wine. Jesus did what His mother wanted him to do. It is interesting thinking of Jesus, since the Bible tells us of the important things He did. There's a lot left out of His life. God made sure the Bible had in it, what we needed to know.

I think about when Jesus left home on His mission. What was Jesus' mission? To tell people about God the Father that sent Him. He was also there to help people. Jesus recruited people to follow him. Some asked if they could go along. They were poor, so they walked most places. Well I thought about sitting around the campfire at night, with the Son of God. I'm sure they were tired from walking in the heat. We are not told about it in the Bible, but I bet it was amazing hanging around with God the Son. Maybe clouds for a little shade, or a little rain. I think it was hard, and they roughed it most of the time, but when you are with Jesus, things can go better.

These followers, called disciples certainly didn't know Jesus was the Son of God early on. They did know that Jesus was special. I'm sure these followers of Jesus saw Him do things that made them wonder and say, Wow!

The Bible tells us that man was made in God's image. So, God knows, and has feelings like us. Happiness, sadness, anger and so on. Of course, these kinds of feelings are different for God than they are for us. God is not human. Sadness, anger or any feeling can overwhelm us, but not God. God can just wish it, and it leaves His mind. You can know for sure; God has lots of joy with His Son sitting next to Him.

God didn't have any problems until He created angels and humans. He gave us all free will, so some angels and all men and women sinned. We were born into sin. You can easily see it on this planet. Well problems just don't get to God; He takes care of problems.

Jesus and His disciples (followers) were on a boat, when a storm came up. Jesus was asleep at the time, and they woke Him because they thought they were going to drown. Jesus told the storm, and waves to stop and it became calm. Miracles like this, I'm sure Jesus followers were realizing who Jesus was.

God sent His Son to our world to do a mission that had to be done. This mission was for us humans and it was because of that He sent His Son Jesus. When man sinned, it took us away from God. Sinful man can't be with a perfect and holy God. Some people really don't care to be perfect. None of us can be perfect. God fixed sin through His Son to make us perfect again.

Some people may think to worship, and praise God for eternity, will be boring. God will not be boring, ever. If you try to imagine wonderful things, well heaven will likely be like that. We know there will be no more sorrow or pain. With God having all power and knowledge we will likely learn from God for an eternity. No doubt it will be nice just to make it to heaven where God is. Eventually there will be a new earth. We will have new bodies. We will eat fruit from the tree of life. I doubt that would matter since we will live for eternity with God. I brought up eating because we won't have to bother with going to the restroom.

We just know for sure that God wants us to be with Him. He wouldn't have created us, and sent His Son Jesus, for us but He did.

Most people still just live their life out on earth, and don't think much about where we came from. We are all a little different in the way we think about life, or a lot different. God is the same as He always has been, He doesn't change. With this mystery of creation and life, you would think more people would think that something is in charge of it all.

Even with an invisible God, I really don't know how people can think it just happened somehow. I'm talking about creation and life. I've mentioned before that most scientists and professors think we evolved from ape. So, it sticks even though they don't know. Like millions of years ago, while the earth was cooling there were soupy pools, and comets bombarded the earth with water, and the building blocks for life. Supposedly one celled amoeba formed in these pools, and all life came from them. Think of all life on this planet and there are so many species. Would not there have to be millions of 1 celled amoebas, one for each different creature. Man had to form also and as we evolve could we see or walk?

Our eyes are so complex they would need to evolve completely, then maybe we could see what to do. I also heard maybe when I went to school, humans likely came from a creature in the ocean, lost its tail and walked out on land. This was much farther back in time before ape to man. I could go on with this stupid theory of the beginning of life on earth, but I won't because it is a stupid theory by people that don't want to bring God into creation. This theory comes from Satan. Satan has been busy not wanting you to believe or know God. God and Satan are enemies. God and Satan are invisible, but God has all power. You can see the work of both God and Satan. The beauty of this world and love is due to God, and the bad in this world and hate is all Satan. God created Satan or Lucifer and gave him free will. Lucifer wanted power like God. God cast Lucifer out of heaven, but Lucifer convinced around a third of angels to go with him. After Lucifer's fall he is called Satan or the devil.

I find it interesting that this all-powerful an all knowing God is focused on this planet earth, and the people on it. Maybe God feels obligated. Since He created us. He had to give us freedom or freewill when He created us. It was the right thing to do, so we can make our own decisions. After sin came into the world, because of Satan and us, God sees a lot of awful and disgusting things on the earth.

God is at work, if you think about it, trying and wanting to save people. He gave us creation and the Bible. So many varieties of life on this planet, that only God could have done it. So, what is people's problem? Mainly we take things for granted. It is easier to believe creation just popped up somehow, like lots of scientists and professors say.

God says it is easy and free to believe and go with God. We know it isn't all that easy. There is really a battle out there. The world is against you believing in God and being a Christian. The world is more for a person to take life for granted, be careful, but sin a little, you'll be OK. Don't make waves.

It is going to get worse. Most people see what is going on in our country and the world. The hate in our country, and our government, is a big part of the problem. We are not strong enough to fight this without God. We have enough trouble understanding it. By the way, I pray for all of you out there.

What is interesting, and marvelous is God wants to help you. Yes you! That individual relationship with you. We see all the problems we have on our planet, and God is thinking of you. It is God's will that you come to Him, and love Him back with your own free will, like He loves you. I don't believe it is God's will to fix the problems on this earth, yet. I know it is God's will to help you, and all of us. We just have to decide that we need help and go to God. That is our decision, and the most important decision in our life. I also believe God allows us to have problems, so we might seek His help. He can help , although we still live on this world of good and bad.

Most people move around on this planet of ours and don't think of important things. Important things like

God, the Bible and creation. Some people do. We have to work and take care of our families. After that we try to enjoy life. There is nothing wrong with that. We should take care of our families and try to enjoy life. I know most people do their own thing, and don't think about God much, or at all. How can God get your attention? Eventually God will have all our attention. I'm sure most people have at least wondered about all creation, and the life we have on this planet. God that always was, and always will be, created everything. Aliens or comets bringing the building blocks for life didn't do it. You would have to ask where did they come from. God has always been around. Always! We have trouble even thinking of always. There's an awesome God out there. The wonderful thing is He is loving and perfect. Because He is an invisible God, people have always had a problem with that. How do we or can we believe in an invisible God? Let's look at some of the things He has done to help us believe. For one thing we are here, and our bodies are amazing. The rest of creation is amazing. God didn't just give us a few trees, a few plants, and a few animals. He could have. God gave us so much life in His creation; we are still discovering new ones. Life underground, life in oceans, rivers, lakes, life on top of the ground, and life in the air. God needed us to understand certain things, so He made sure we had the Bible. Some people disregard the Bible or don't believe it. I would have to say do you not believe the wisdom in the Bible. How about how He made man and woman perfectly, speaking a language and intelligent. We didn't evolve. How about all the prophecies that come true and will continue to come true. Only God can tell of future events or can make future events happen. There are hundreds of prophecies in the Bible. Check it out; God will not let one prophecy get by Him. They will all come true. Sure, creation and life is a mystery, but us humans like good mysteries. God and creation is less of a mystery than what science wants to tell us. First off, they will say they are not sure. They say we came or evolved from apes. God says He made man perfectly in His image. Man could figure and spoke a language. Actually, God the Trinity made man. The Bible says, let us make man in our image. We are special because God breathed the breath of life into us. Not just for Adam and Eve, but everyone.

Ecclesiastes 11: 5

Just as you don't know how the breath of life enters the limbs of a child within its mother's womb, you also don't understand how God who made everything works.

God loves us all. You might wonder if He loves bad people. God loves all of His creation; He just doesn't love what they do. What is bad and good? We understand it, but it is really talked about in the Bible. The Bible is really the only place that bad and good is talked about. The bad is called sin. The Bible is full of stories of sinful people. Sin is probably talked about more than anything in the Bible. Why? This God of ours wants as many that will, come and live with Him for eternity. That is what God wants, and that is amazing. He sent His Son Jesus to make it happen.

The Bible is amazing. It has a little bit of everything in it since it deals with life. It tells us history of people and God. It is something you really have to study a little, because it is not all easy to understand. God is not easy to understand. What He wants us to know, is easy to understand. He wants us to know about His Son Jesus. He wants us to know that Jesus came to fix the sin problem. It is wonderful, and amazing what God has done for us. We think of Jesus more now because He is our way back to God. This three in one God work together to help humans. We can call this three in one God just God. We do have an amazing, and all-powerful God. There are many people that love God and are trying to help. God and these helpers are wanting to get your attention. People have to make a choice, to put their life in the hands of Jesus, or not. We all live on this earth, and none of us are, or will be perfect. We need help and forgiveness because we will fail sometimes.

Well think about why only the Bible tells us so much about good and bad. There is so much more in the Bible that makes perfect sense. Most scientists and professor's ideas of creation makes no sense. They are not sure anyway. God's creation that is talked about in the Bible, God is sure. God having all power, and all knowledge, makes some things maybe seem unbelievable to some people. God can do anything. God can wipe people out, and still be a perfect God. What God creates He can get rid of, it belongs to Him. We push God, to shaking His head for sure. Millions of abortions, killings, the sin just goes on and on , on this planet. Isn't it wonderful God is merciful?

I believe the worst sin people do, is not acknowledging God. He has done so much for His creation, man, but most men and women don't believe. Many do believe, and their life on this planet is better just because they believe in God the Father, God the Son and God the Holy Spirit. These people have the same problems non-believers have. We all live on this planet with the good and bad. I should add Satan in the mix. If you lean on God, Satan won't be bothering you. Christians have something to look forward to; eternal life with God.

God knew we would have problems, so He gave us the Bible. The Bible is a miracle in itself, it can't be proven to be a lie. The Bible talks about the world getting worse as time goes by. The division and hate is a big problem. Jesus said we should love God and love one another. What has happened to our leaders, our government? Lots of people in our country want people to think like them. I don't understand people like that. In a free country it should be OK to think how you want. Some hate other people, that don't think like they want. It is crazy.

Jesus said seek and you will find, knock and the door will be opened. It seems simple, and it is, but we have to walk through the door. Many of us just do our own thing, with our free will God gave us. Through time, I'm sure we all have done our own thing. I did for a long time, and I believe I was a Christian.

There is plenty of sin on this earth, so many have to keep knocking on the door, and the door keeps opening. We have to walk through the door and then we can have a personal relationship With God. That is what God wants. The Bible says God loves us, every one of us. He is the Creator, and our heavenly Father. Being our heavenly Father and Creator, He wants us to do what is right and not sin. Well we are weak, and we live on the earth with plenty of sinful things to do.

God knew we wouldn't be able to be perfect when He gave us free will. God has always been trying to help people not to sin. He talks about it all through the Bible.

Like the wages for sin is death. God set a high standard. With a caring God, why do we have to hurt and mourn when our loved ones die? So we live, and die, and that is it. Remember God loves us, so death is not it. God loves us so much, He came up with a plan. He didn't have to figure out the plan; He knew what had to happen. A sinless and wonderful God had to come to this earth, and willingly die in our place. Jesus did that, God the Son and took the sin of the world on himself. That is a lot more love than we can imagine. It was a perfect plan that only God could accomplish it. Jesus suffered big time, for us He didn't miraculously get rid of the pain. He was flesh like us, and He was God. Well He died, and they placed him in a tomb. His Father God raised him back to life. God the Father was very pleased with His Son, Jesus.

Remembering that God the Father, God the Son, and God the Holy Spirit are one, well God the Son came to this earth to die in our place. Did God die in our place, in the form of man, and was beaten half to death and nailed to a cross? Yes! That is a lot of love, to do that for us.

Most people have heard of Satan. You can bet he was not pleased with this plan of Gods'. This may all sound like a fantasy story, but the plan, or mission Jesus came to do was perfect. God only does perfect things. Satan, the world, or no one can say that God the Son, giving up

His life to take away sin from man, isn't good enough. It is just amazing that He did this for us. God says, those that believe this mission that Jesus took care of, will be saved. Jesus had to do this for us; we can do little living on this sinful planet. Without Jesus, and what He did for us, we can't be with God. If you think of man and woman, what an amazing thing we are. Think of the other creatures on this earth. Some of them are smarter than others. But man and woman are very intelligent compared to the creatures on this earth. So, is there more than us? I would certainly hope so, and we should all feel that there is. The more than us, is invisible to us, but they are there in one amazing God. We should all think of ourselves. To be human, and where did we come from, and for what reason are we here? Again, I will say, most people just take everything for granted. I said we should think of ourselves. Usually that is a bad way to think. When it comes to God, there's only you and God. God loves everyone but He deals with people one at a time. It is interesting that God can deal with people one at a time and still deal with millions one at a time, at the same time. Time is important to man, but God is outside of time. Time means nothing to God, but He knows when our time runs out.

You know, God says when He sees believers, those that love Him, and believe in what His Son Jesus did He only sees the blood of Jesus. That is interesting. God can will himself not to see our sins, ever. The blood of Jesus wipes out sins and that was Jesus' mission on earth. That is what He did.

We can't understand fully about a lot of things, and that is why the Bible talks a lot about faith. God and His Son Jesus, made promises to us. It is a good time to remind people of what Jesus said to Thomas, one of Jesus' followers. Thomas is known as doubting Thomas. After Jesus was crucified, and died His followers were very depressed. I guess being human they didn't think what Jesus had said to them and the times He brought people back to life. They heard Jesus was alive again and they took it in different ways. Thomas said he would have to see the wounds in Jesus before he believed. Jesus showed up in the room where His followers were. He didn't come in through the door, He was just there with them. Jesus showed Thomas His wounds. He said to Thomas, "you believe because you see , blessed are those that believe, but haven't seen".

We are to have faith in what God, and His Son Jesus said they would do. Faith in believing that there is God at all, is less necessary. We have much proof of God already. There are hundreds of prophecies in the Bible. Besides creation, us, and the Bible itself, prophecies are proof of God. Who makes predictions come true hundreds, to thousands of years later? Only God knows, or makes the future happen.

Isaiah 42:8-9 I am the Lord that is my name I will not give my glory to anyone else or the praise I deserve to idols. What I said in the past has come true. I will reveal new things before they happen.

God is talking through prophets, or to His chosen people.

Isaiah 46:8-11

Remember this and take courage. Recall your rebellious acts. Remember the first events, because I am God, and there is no other. I am God, and there's no one like me. From the beginning I revealed the end. From long ago I told you things that had not yet happened, saying my plan would stand, and I'll do everything I intended to do. I will call a bird of prey from the east. I will call someone for my plan from a faraway land. I have spoken and I will bring it about. I have planned it and I will do it.

This was some verses about God talking about His prophecies, and that He alone is in control of what will happen.

I'll say again that I'm writing this book because we humans are special on this earth. I think we all can see that. Everything was set up for us to have a life on this planet. I'm sure that most people occasionally wonder how we got here. How did all of this come to be, and what is the goal to all of it. There is too much to it for there to be no goal to it. What is the point if we are all dead and gone eventually? I believe our personal goal is to make our way to the Creator, God. I also know He is waiting for many to come to Him. He is not going to wait too much longer. We can see this by what the country, and the world looks like. The hate and division is ruining our country. The Bible talks about all of this mess. It calls it sin. Hate and sin seems to be winning out over love. The Bible is making more sense, as every day goes by.

In writing this book I've been looking at the Bible, God's Word more closely. I've seen things that are amazing like all the prophecies.

God gave us the Bible, since creation without the Bible; we just take everything for granted. I care about the children, especially those that don't live in a Christian home. Most people don't check out the Bible, since it has been around over a thousand years. Where else can we find out about life, and death and everything in between? The Bible is the only place. Most people don't believe in the Bible, and most of them don't know what is in the Bible. God wanted us to understand certain things, so He gave us the Bible. He wanted us to know the truth about creation. He wanted us to understand about life and death, right and wrong, and the way to get back to the Father God. God especially wanted us to know about His Son Jesus. Jesus is the way, the truth, and the life. No one can get to the Father God, except through Jesus. This is why Jesus is known as the savior of the world.

God is perfect, so we can't be with God as sinners. We are all sinners. God sent His Son to fix that problem. He fixed it. Jesus went through a lot, and death to fix the sin problem. You think God could have fixed this sin problem another way, since He has all power? It took a blood sacrifice from God, to save us from all sin in the world.

There are hundreds of predictions of Jesus' coming to this earth, hundreds and thousands of years before He came. Only God could do that. Only God tells us of things to come in the future, and He has done it all through the Bible.

The Bible is not something you could make up. If you could you wouldn't want to bore readers about family lineages. Like this family were so and so and had three sons. Their names were so and so. Pages like that, but it just proves the Bible also. It is called history of people. God wanted us to have the Bible, and we do. We humans can believe in it, or not. So, we have the freedom to believe the universe, and the abundance of life on this beautiful planet just popped up somehow or God and the Bible are a true fact!

If there were no trees on this planet, or wildflowers and tomorrow there were, what would you think? You would think Creator, or Supreme Being or God. If God took away our taking things for granted, what would we think? I'm sure we would marvel about all of creation. We take so much for granted.

Many of us take our cell phones, and IPads for granted, and what would many do without them? How about Facebook and Twitter, what if it was gone? Let's just say a lot of people couldn't handle that.

We tend to take God for granted, since He is invisible. Everything visible came from God. Creation happened long ago, so people take it for granted. We are born into it. I don't say God gave us cell phones, or IPads. Everything man makes came from this planet that God created, and from our hands, and minds that God created.

Whether people believe in God, or not we have a lot in creation that is a mystery. Like I've mentioned before, many scientists and professors don't help much with this mystery. They just don't know and can't know.

They talk about a "big bang" in empty space, and the soupy pools where they say likely comets brought the building blocks for life. Later we get to the ape to man theory. These are all theories from learned people, and shame on them. Why shame on them? Because those theories seem to stick. Our children learn these theories. Museums around the country shows the ape to man theory. The same museums where you can see dinosaur bones. Dinosaur bones are real, but ape to man is only a theory. If you can think of these things, think of a war between God and Satan. Satan was certainly involved in the theory of ape to man. If people don't believe in Satan, well he sure is keeping people on this planet from believing in God. It is strange, but think about that Satan wants you and God wants you. The difference is huge. Satan doesn't care about you at all, he just wants to keep you away from God. God, on the other hand loves you, and has given you the way to live in paradise with Him forever. People that don't believe in God or Satan, still have to acknowledge good and bad in our world. What side is winning do you think? The good or the bad? You can just not think about these things, and most people on our planet don't.

Think of the past on our planet, long before our time. Egypt worshipped the sun god, and many other gods. Other countries worshipped the sun. Everything people worshipped back then the one God created. Whether people believe in God or not, we know there can only be one God. If there were more than one, the battle wouldn't last long, because the one God has all power and wisdom. It is OK to think about things like that because God wants you to think about Him. I think about Him a lot, in writing this book. I'll just say He is an amazing God.

I'm going to think of creation again, because a few weeks ago I saw a walking stick on the screen door. I don't know the scientific name for this creature, but I'm sure most people have seen one . It does look like a twig with eyes. Only God can think of creatures like this. I'm sure we can think of creatures we don't like, like mosquitoes, flies and other things. When sin came into the world long ago, we get the bad stuff. We can now add corona virus to the bad. I wonder what else will happen?

I think if we were able to get rid of all the bad in the world, we would have a perfect world. God says He originally made the world perfect. Do you think about these things? If you do, you have to think about God. God thinks about you.

In writing about God, here I am writing about walking sticks, wildflowers, Satan, sin, we humans, and everything else. Well, that is our God. Sometimes I just stare out the window in awe of this powerful God.

The mystery to me, I think of after 9/11, the terrorist attack. Many more people went to church. All wars cause people to cry out to God. After these things pass, so does the crying out to God. When someone gets injured anytime, they usually cry out to God. Sometimes it is a curse word using God's name. They still cry out to God. I think God put this in us, to help us. It is like whether we want it or not, we have a feeling of God. Since we were very young God knew us, and even before we were ever born.

To bring up Satan again, which I don't like to, well, God wants me to. Satan wants us all to take everything for granted. Satan sometimes works in people's minds. He has power to do that. He wants us to believe that God is not real. He wants us to believe we evolved from an ape. Lies, hate, and deception is his domain. He only has so much power over us, only what God allows Him to have.

We have to remember there is an extreme good in the world, and that is God. We wonder about this good, and bad in the world. Some really don't need Satan's help to do bad.

Most people have what is called common sense. We know what is right, and wrong. Then I think of our government. Is it what is wrong is right, and what is right is racist? They like to use certain words, and we can barely understand them. I mean understand these people, and media and protestors. I'm just a simple American that cares, so here is another verse from our God.

Job 34:19

Who shows no partiality to princes nor regards the rich over the poor, for they are all the work of his hands.

We all have occasional problems on this earth. I should say this good, and bad earth. We all grew up knowing that there are problems, here and there in life. God's Word says it wasn't meant to be that way.

If you think about it, and the Bible talks about it, we have a battle going on this earth between good and evil. Also, right and wrong, and truth and lies. God has the power to do what is needed but like through past till now He wants to see what we do. Do we stand for God, and help Him, or not? God doesn't need help if He wanted to destroy all sinners on this earth, but He doesn't. He is a God of love.

Love is a big, and important word and Jesus talked a lot about it. The other side of love is hate and we have more and more of that in our world. The news on TV is mostly hate and lies. Hate and lies go hand in hand.

The same one that tempted Eve and Adam is at work on our planet. That is Satan. Like I said before he is the one that should have his picture over ape to man, in our museums. Taking our minds off of the Creator, God, is what he wants. Satan, the Bible says is the great liar, and wants us to take life and creation for granted. I know you can't see God or Satan, so they don't exist, huh? You don't see the wind, and we can't make a tree, or the seed it grew from.

I should add, why am I writing a book that I never thought to do and calling it God. I couldn't do this without His help.

Anyone out there can stand up for God, even a sinner, and a sinner like me, and all of us. Many of us sinners have gone to God, and He can help us. We know of Jesus, and He helps us.

I know many on earth think, to get close to God; you can't really have fun anymore. Is that true? I think that is more of Satan's trickery. If you were to make a list of good and bad things that are fun, not many fun things are bad.

The Holy Spirit helps Christians and with this world and our country getting worse and worse we need help.

If you join the battle for good, I call it, that can be fun and interesting. The world might be against you, but the one that has all power will be for you. Go to God, and He will help you, and put meaning in your life. Don't be impatient in talking to God. We humans want something to happen right away. Just going to God will make you feel good. I believe that is humans calling, to seek the Creator. He created you, and all creation belongs to God. Give yourself back to God.

In the time I've been writing this book about God, and what God must feel about us humans, things seem to get worse and worse. Corona virus, more and more hate, protests and division. What about defunding and getting rid of police. What about common sense? This book is needed but will it help? This country was amazing, and I say was, because I'm very concerned. Some want to destroy this country, and some leaders are ok with that. Most of us can't understand people like this. There aren't really any answers to it all; and our government is a mess.

There are good and bad people on this earth, and they may be in law enforcement, in the military, in schools, or anywhere. We are all different, and some are better than others. As long as we all live on this earth with good and bad on it, there will be problems. This country was set up to be better, policemen, and laws, protection and common sense.

People are like when they need God, they call on Him, when He doesn't do what people want immediately, they are not pleased. Not that we are mad at God, but why call on Him? God the creator, rarely gets a call from most people, and doesn't even get recognized as God. Of course, God is not like people and is always the same. God has common sense. We are just weak compared to God.

God created us and loves us all the same. Like I said before He just doesn't like the sin, we do. So why is the word racist, and other words used now, and especially by our own government. There have been mistakes made in the past, but now it is over power and importance. God doesn't see your power and importance. God certainly doesn't care about skin color. I don't believe people think of skin color, maybe some, but very few.

Mankind's goal should be to seek the Creator - God.

We are the only country that tried to build a country putting God first. Like one nation under God, and in God we trust. Like God given rights like, liberty, freedom, and the pursuit of happiness. No one, and no country is perfect. We are still the best country in the world. Our country and a lot of the people, don't look to God like in the past. Some Christians I know have wondered if God has taken His blessings off of America. America is sick with many problems and the rest of the world also. I know God blesses many people that love Him. God works with people individually.

God sees all, and these protests of chaos and cruelty, well I feel bad that God has to see it. The abortions that America sends to God, and so many more bad things, well the country is just sick. I still love the country. I know God does also, but He doesn't like the evil in the country. Things could be fixed with God's help, but most people don't even acknowledge God, and take creation for granted.

I care about people, and pray they quit taking creation for granted. You first have to think about it. To see everything that man couldn't make on this planet is vast. There was a time years ago when man lived without grocery stores, without automobiles, and without Facebook, and the luxuries of life. God put everything on this planet, for man to survive. Since we were given intelligence from God, we have come so far, we don't need God anymore. Is that true? Certainly not! We haven't conquered death. God has, and He sent His Son Jesus to do it. It was all for us.

The Bible tells us the world is going to get messed up, more and more. Do you see what is happening? Our government is a joke. They don't get along, and they have completely different philosophies on how they want the world, or country to be. It seems they don't care about the people or the country. They mostly want power over all of us, but they need the vote, and they will do almost anything to get it.

What is important in this world? The answer to that is another question. Who does the universe belong to? Humans and everything belong to the Creator, God.

God didn't make some humans better than other humans. We know that some people are better educated, some are richer than others, some have more power than others, and you can think of more. Also, some think they are closer to God than others. We also hear of racism, and that is just the color of a person's skin. This is all ridiculous, and people should respect, and appreciate everyone else because they were created by God. If you happen to be born perfect and grow up to be good looking, smart and powerful, are you better than a person that is born with problems, and grows up in pain? No! God says He loves us all, and we don't understand why some have a good life, and some don't. We all live on a flawed world because of sin. God loves us all the same since we are His creation. Only God can make us better people, through His Son Jesus. Living on this sinful world, even people that have God in their lives, have to be careful. We can act like we are closer to God than others. Then we tell people about Jesus, like we should, but you act closer to God, than the person you talk to. There are many out there, that need to get there chin down out of the air. We are not all good at talking to people about Jesus. We can still help people. We know that most people don't want you talking to them about God, or Jesus. Why? It is mostly because they know you want to change their life. It has to come from God, and God does want you to change. He wants you to do His will. He is the Creator, and has all power, and all knowledge. He knows what is best for us all, and that is to be with Him in eternity. If we do God's will, we can't have fun anymore. Some or a lot of people feel that way. If you made a list of all the fun things you enjoy doing, likely 99% of them are not sinful. God created a beautiful world and there are lots of enjoyments out there. So actually, you are leaving the best thing out of your life, when you worry about not having fun anymore, God! If you don't try to know God, what are you missing out on? You don't know, because you don't know God . God has to cause excitement and happiness in people's lives, when we live on a world that is getting worse and worse. He is the only one that can. He is completely in charge of everything. He wants you to think of it this way, He loves you. He is not like the world, and He is not like us humans. He is not human like us but He created us. Who can create us? He is amazing!

If you subtract the sin, and bad things from the world, you see what God intended for us. No death and no sorrow either.

God put so many prophecies in the Bible, some that happened thousands of years ago , some that happened more recent and some, like about Israel and the Jews sixty to seventy years ago. God causes and makes these prophecies come true. Many prophecies haven't happened yet, but they will. God does not fail. Why are all the prophecies in the Bible? God knows it is not easy for us, having an invisible God. Who lets us know, who predicts the future? God and only God. It is proof of God and the Bible. People either are not going to think about it, and I mean prophecy and God, or they are too busy. Some day that prophecy, by God is going to catch up to us all and we will have to recognize God's Word.

It is not easy to talk to people about God, but if we don't, we will be partially responsible for people not knowing God. Of course, most people don't really want you talking to them about God. That is the way the world is for some reason, and another victory for Satan.

There is a true story in my hometown, years ago about the pastor of a church talking to a wino on the street.

Someone from the church said it didn't look good for this pastor talking to the wino. Jesus in His time hung around many sinners. These sinners needed most of the help. We are all sinners, but through God we can help others. Time is slowly running out. Just watch the news on TV for a few minutes, and you get the message.

Some people in the country and the world shy away from Christians. It is just the way of the world. That is another victory of Satan. Christians are not better than anyone else, and we know God loves us all the same. I don't mean to get in trouble with Christians because I am one. Christians are different than non-Christians. Christians believe in God and His Son Jesus and what He did for us all. He saved us from our sins. It is a free gift from God. We Christians want to do God's will and God does help us through His Holy Spirit. We live on this world of good and bad, so Christians also fail sometimes. So don't worry about Christians. We mess up like all the rest of you. Another difference is we have an all-powerful God that wants to help us, and He does. We also want to please God; we have to think what He has done for us. What His Son Jesus did for us, and everyone out there?

God gets glory from all creation and He deserves glory. Every time a sinner seeks God and His Son, He gets more glory.

I like to write about happy things, but in this life on earth we don't have all happiness. Our children can certainly bring happiness, sometimes of course.

Children sometimes ask their parents where did God come from, or who made God? Sadly, some children in their family may not hear of God. Anyway, where did God come from? That is an interesting question at any age. If God has been around forever, what was He doing before creation? He had joy with a companion Godhead, His Son Jesus and the Holy Spirit

God lives outside of time, so time didn't start until creation. So wondering what God was doing before creation, is something not answerable. But God always was and always will be.

I'm going to write about something people wonder about. Aliens and UFO's. I believe there is something to it. Before creation, do you think God could have created elsewhere, or more civilizations? That is God's business, and He could have. Too many people have seen UFO's, and cave drawings, and other unexplainable things. I don't know if I believe in it or not. All I know is God is in charge, and if there are aliens, we don't need to be concerned. I do know if there are aliens, they are different than us. We were made in God's image. Jesus wouldn't be going to one civilization and dying for their sins, and then another and another. There are just things we don't understand. Some documentaries on TV, they talk about maybe aliens had something to do with creating humans or changing our DNA to make us what we are. Then the mystery would just go on, since you would have to wonder who created them? God told us what we needed to know. He gave us a Bible.

I watch the news probably more than I should, but I'm curious to know what is going on now. It is depressing but I know the news has always been about the bad stuff going on in the world. So it tells me a lot, because it is getting worse. If you think of God, you can still smile.

When I was a kid you didn't hear about our government much. I didn't watch news much then, but older people and my parents didn't talk about the government. Today what the government is doing, is the talk, and on the news constantly. It is lots of division and hate. We really need God. God that makes the seed, apples and oranges.

Like I said before, I wished and prayed that God would help somehow. I know He wants us to help , and I realize that God has been at work trying to get people's attention. God does have lots of help. Most people are just living their life on this planet, and not recognizing God. If you don't ever recognize God, He won't be a part of your life.

In my writing about God, I have to write about sin and problems we have. God is the only one that can help, and I know He is helping with my writing. You might wonder why I know He is helping me write. A lot of things in this book just came to my head that I didn't seem to think about, but I liked it. I also didn't even think about writing a book. I did think that the country and the world needed God's help. He loves us all, and why wouldn't He help me write this? Like I said before, He wants to get your attention. He uses lots of people to help get His message out there.

I would rather write about the beauty in God's creation and the abundance of creation. I have to write about sin and neglecting God also. If we could subtract the bad in the world, we would have a perfect world. Only in the Bible, God's Word tells us about creation and Satan tempting Eve and Adam, He fixed the problem through His Son Jesus.

God wants His creation, humans to be with Him for eternity. That is interesting. We have to choose God, if we don't, we automatically choose the world. Life is short and there is no one on this planet that can help. Help in understanding life, only God can help. He did by giving us the Bible. Why does the Bible tell us so much about life and creation? Nowhere else can we get that information. Scientists and professors give us some information on how they think creation could have happened. They at least say that they are not sure. There is no way for them to be sure. The Bible tells us of things to come, in prophecies. There are many prophecies of things that have already happened. It hasn't been wrong yet. There are prophecies all through the Bible and that is proof of God. Only God knows the future and He also makes future events come true.

To think of God having all power, and knowledge means He can do anything He wants to. The prophecies in the Bible have a perfect record of being true. There are many prophecies in the Bible of Jesus' coming to this earth. Some of them talk about His miraculous birth, and some about what He would do here. It is amazing and some prophecies of Jesus were hundreds of years and thousands of years before He came here. You would think people would want to check out these prophecies in the Bible. When I was writing this book, I was very surprised in all of these prophecies. They are proof of God! Like I said before prophecies are much easier to find in the Bible now. You can use the internet to find them. There are prophecies of other things. Many prophecies of Israel and the Jewish people. They were, and are God's chosen people. The Bible talks about the Jews being dispersed throughout the world. Since they were God's chosen people, they paid a price for going against God. We know what Hitler did to many of them in World War Two. It was predicted that they would return to their promised land. They won't be dispersed again. The world and especially Christians keep their eye on this little country of Israel. Why? Because the Bible says they are God's chosen people. I will write a prophecy by God about his chosen people.

Jeremiah 31: 10 written about 600 BC Hear the Word of the Lord, you nations listen to the Word of the Lord. Tell it to the distant islands. Say, the one who scattered the people of Israel will gather them and watch over them as a Shepherd watches over his flock. The Lord will free the descendants of Jacob and reclaim them from those who are stronger than they are.

Leviticus 26: 11 -12 I will put my tent among you, and I will never look at you with disgust. So I will live among you and be your God, and you will be my people.

There are many of these prophecies, and the ones about the Jews and Israel are much more recent. They have been blessed. They grow lots of things, enough to export some. They do have countries around them that don't care much for them. I pray and hope for peace there. I know Israel will be OK, they have a powerful ally

To read these prophecies about Israel, that happened much more recent. The Jews, in Israel are here on this planet, so things continue to happen, and we can see it. It is interesting. Israel and the Jews are proof of the prophecies about them.

All humans on this planet fail God; it wasn't just the Jewish people that messed up. Since they were, and are God's chosen people, thousands of years ago they kept going against God's wishes, and they were dispersed through much of the world. God warned them. Now they are back, God has forgiven them and they won't lose their land again. God says He is with them. That is a big reason why Christians, keep an eye on Israel. It is all proof of God.

America is a different situation than Israel, but we were blessed like them. We made a country, one nation under God, and in God we trust. We put God first, and we flourished. We are now farther from God. As time goes by, we neglect God and don't pay attention to Him. God hasn't changed, and never will, we do change. The country is changing. It is changing for the worse. Look at our government, and you see a real mess. The people in the country are bad, good, and all in between. Some people want things for nothing, some don't want to do anything. A country can't stand very well with people that don't care, and people with lots of hate. There are still many in the country that work hard and care.

Like how we started this country, one nation under God, we need to get back to that. We all need to lean on God.

Most of us work, and wonder what is going to happen next. We all have to go through this life, with the burden on our shoulders of a country, and government falling apart. The latest things, corona virus, protestors destroying everything they can, and defunding the police. You know it is bad when a lot of the leaders go along with all of that. I'm just another working American out here, that is shocked by it all. I wonder what is going to happen next, and something else does. There is lots of hate out there. It looks like I will keep getting new material for this book.

I'm writing about God and how He feels about us humans on this earth. Most people have to know how God feels about it. I feel bad that God has to see all the nonsense, hate, and just plain evil happening on this earth. What did Jesus say when He was on this earth? He said the most important commandment was to love God, and to love one another. That statement makes more and more sense every day. All I can say is God is watching. I write about this because I also know that God will eventually get fed up.

God loves his creation so much, us, that He wants to give time for more and more people to know Him.

Many on this planet take creation as something that just happened. Some people are full of hate, and some just don't care one way or the other. I'm sorry for these people, and pray for them, because they will likely not seek God. I don't like to make things sound bad, but this world does it without my saying it. I know God wants me to say it.

Think of all the things man has made on this planet. We have made many things that make a better and easier life for us. The list of things man has made goes on and on. We even went to the moon. We were given the hands, bodies and minds from the Creator, God. Everything we used to make things came from this earth. We can't make a seed, or an apple, or a tree. That is what God does. What God has created just goes on and on. We get caught up in all the things men have made. We need to quit taking creation for granted and think about all the beauty on this earth. The beauty that only God can make and He made it for us.

If you think about creation and God, things get interesting. We still have the mystery of things we don't understand. People have always liked things interesting and mysterious.

I remind people and I know God wants me to, about creation and God. People seem to need continuous reminding, since most people take everything for granted. So, I'll say some things over and over in this book. Things like we are moving through space around the sun at approximately 67,000 miles per hour. We are the perfect distance from the sun for life on this planet. There shouldn't be any doubt, that only God sets up the world. How He sets things up for us is amazing. He didn't have to put so much beauty, but He did.

The wildflowers, sunsets, and so much beauty He put here because He can. He has all power and knowledge, and He loves us. God is a mystery to most people, but what He made you can see and it is all simply amazing.

Even God has an enemy. I wouldn't bring him up, but he causes problems on this earth. He is known as a great liar, and he is jealous of God. He is also invisible, Satan, and he has power since he is an angel. A fallen angel that we didn't need. You don't have to believe in Satan since man can sin without Satan's help, and we do. Satan tries to do things to keep people from believing in God. He is out to keep as many from God as he can. That is plain evil and mean. By the way Satan can't create anything, only God has that power. The mystery is, why didn't God wipe Satan out? I guess it wasn't in God's plan, yet. The Bible talks a lot about this evil angel.

I'm just writing about all of this, I think if people try to add up all of creation, you would come up with an all-powerful God. Plants, animals, birds, underground creatures and underwater creatures, we couldn't add them up in a lifetime. So did it just all happen somehow? No way! We are smarter than that. Look how the universe is set up. If you could figure all of creation, and think of how it was set up for life, it just goes on and on. How about us humans to top it off, we are very incredible creatures on this earth, putting it lightly. To not think a creator, God, had to do all of this, is what Satan wants us to think. Satan can't and doesn't create, he destroys. He is doing well in keeping people from believing in God. One thing Satan is good at is like pushing the ape to man theory. He will get involved in anything that will cause men to doubt God. Of course, man doesn't always need help to doubt God. Satan knows God and believes in Him because he was with God. God created Satan and he was called Lucifer. He was to be a helper to God. Satan was not content and wanted more power. Most people don't believe in Satan, and if you figure the whole world, most people don't believe in Satan or God. We have a dilemma then, and a problem. Like creation that couldn't have just happened, and things set up perfectly for life on this planet that points to a Creator God. We have bad, or evil that point to Satan, the devil. Yes, it is a mystery, and interesting. Think of all the things Satan has done on this planet to keep our minds off of God. We humans do a good job of keeping our minds off of God, all by ourselves. We do have to admit that more and more problems are happening in our country, and the world.

Problems are written about and prophesized in the Bible. Again, I'll say, people don't pay attention and take creation for granted. The Bible proves God, and God proves the Bible, through his prophecy. Only God can tell of future events. We should all consider these Bible verses from God, which I will write out some.

Isaiah 42: 8-9

I am the Lord, that is my name. I will not give my glory to anyone else or the praise I deserve to idols. What I said in the past has come true, I will reveal new things before they happen.

Isaiah 41 :21-24

Present your case says the Lord. Bring forward your best arguments says Jacob 's king. Bring your idols so they can tell us what's going to happen. Explain past events that your idols told you about so that we may consider them and know what their outcome will be. Tell us about future events, tell us what's going to happen so that we may know that you are gods. Yes, do something good or evil to intimidate us, and make us afraid. You are nothing. Whoever chooses you is disgusting.

Isaiah 46:8-11 Remember this and take courage. Recall your rebellious acts. Remember the first events because I am God, and there is no other. I am God and there is no one like me. From the beginning I revealed the end. From long ago I told you things that had not yet happened, saying my plan would stand, and I'll do everything I intended to do, I will call a bird of prey from the east. I will call someone for my plan from a faraway land. I have spoken and I will bring it about. I have planned it, and I will do it.

These three verses that I wrote down are words from God. They show that God is very passionate about His prophecies. If one prophecy doesn't happen, we would doubt the Bible, and doubt God. There are so many prophecies in the Bible, and God will see to it they all happen.

I know many people on this earth don't think much about the Bible, or God. God knew it would be this way, but He loves us and crammed the Bible with many prophecies. You should check it out, because only God can predict the future, and He makes things happen. Anything He wants to do, He can do. Why is it that even with all these prophecies in the Bible, most people on this planet don't pay attention to God? That is another mystery to me, since the Bible is easy to check out. People just don't take the time, or there are better things to do. Are there better things to do than to find out, and know you, and everything was created by God?

I went on the internet to find prophecies in the Bible for this book. I put the Bible beside me to look them up. Some of you can read from the computer, but it is good to read straight from the Bible. I didn't know there were so many. I was very surprised. These prophecies are all proof of God. Having an invisible God, He knew we would need much proof of him. Well these prophecies give it to us. People can't predict, or make future events happen. God has been doing it since the beginning of time.

There are some countries that don't allow the Bible or belief in God. We can only pray, some things are in God's hands. The problem in this world is the same. We have sin in our world and Satan.

If you believe in God, and that He loves us, then His intention was not for us to die. We didn't need to mourn and hurt. Satan caused the first humans to sin, so now we are living with sin and death. God warned man, but He gave us free will to do His will or not.

We were made in God's image, and He will never die. He didn't create us to die. Whether you believe or not,

God said He fixed the problem of sin in our lives. For some reason God wants as many that will, to be with Him For eternity. That is a mystery like creation. You have to say, it is very nice of God to want us to be with Him for eternity. Do you really think we have life, and death on this planet, and a short time in between? Eventually we will all be gone. Just common sense has to let us know, there must be something more than that. Why do humans have minds that feel like there should be more than just life, and death?

Why does our inner being, or spirit not age like the body does? There are many questions about life, and creation God supplied us with answers, He gave us the Bible, and He needed to. We have questions even with the Bible. God gave us answers of what He wanted us to know. Again, think of all the prophecies in the Bible. There are hundreds and they all will come true.

Think of how everything was set up on this earth, and the universe, and think of the Bible telling us about it.

A seed from a plant will grow the same plant. Man can't make a seed. Animals have babies of the same kind. Apes and humans have babies of exactly what they are.

Most of us have enough common sense to know we didn't evolve from an ape. It is a good time to write a verse again from the Bible.

Ecclesiastics 11:5

Just as you don't know how the breath of life enters the limbs of a child, within its mother's womb, you also don't understand how God, who made everything, works.

If you think we evolved from an ape, go back millions of years, like scientists would say, think what the ape had to evolve from. That is where you get to where early man lost its tail and came out of the sea, or pool onto land. While still evolving this creature that had to end up as an ape, had to go through stages of looking very grotesque. God made it hard for this kind of thinking. He created millions of creatures, and millions of different plant life. God said He created man and it was very good. Man was made in God's image, and man was created intelligent, and had a language. Sure, you can listen to what scientists and professors teach about creation, and how the universe was set up. They teach exactly what Satan wants you to think, that there is no God, and everything just happened somehow. To be fair some scientists and professors believe God was the creator, but most don't. I think they mostly believe in their studies, and don't give God any credit. Shame!

Satan believes in God, he was with God, but also had free will and wanted power like God. He was not content with how God created him. He was created to be a top angel, you could say, but wanted more. Satan was cast to earth, and we didn't need that. I know He gets into the minds of people, like scientists and professors, and others to convince us that there is no God. Like I've said, Satan and God are enemies. God wants as many that will, live with Him for eternity. Satan, by lie, trickery or any other way, wants to keep as much of us away from knowing God. If you don't believe in Satan, you can see His works, on this planet. If you don't believe in the Creator, God then again that is proof of Satan.

With over 300 prophecies of Jesus' coming to this earth, in the Old Testament, and predicted hundreds to thousands of years before Jesus was born on earth, you have to figure the most important prophecies in the Bible was that Jesus, the Son of God, was coming. These prophecies also talked about what Jesus would do on this earth. He came to this earth to save mankind from their sins. People that don't believe in God, may not get much out of these prophecies, since they came true over 2000 years ago. The thing is these prophecies just go on and on, all through the Bible. God put so many prophecies throughout the Bible for you, and me, to show that He alone is God. Many prophecies are about God's chosen people, the Jews, and those prophecies can't be denied, because the Jews are still here in Israel. You have to ask yourself, why is that little sliver of a country important to the world? Why do Christians pay close attention to Israel? God gave that land to the Hebrews (Jews) thousands of years ago.

The Jews were dispersed throughout the world for not doing God's will. Of course, we are all guilty of not doing God's will. The Jews were also taken by foreign countries thousands of years ago. They worshiped idols, and did other things, so being God's chosen people, they paid a price. They were scattered and the world didn't treat them well. We know what Hitler did to them during World War II Well it is all over. In 1948 they became a country again. They came back and reclaimed their land. There are still more, and more of them going back. All of these things were prophesized in the Bible. When they came back to Israel, they certainly had problems. For one thing the land was desert and swamps. It is now like a garden. They have flourished and are a powerful country. It wasn't easy for the Jews being that most countries around Israel don't want them there. They had wars and won even when they had very little to fight with, at the time. What they did have was a powerful ally, God. God doesn't change, and the Jews are still God's chosen people. You should do a little research on the Jews.

Even with an ally, God, the Jews in Israel have problems, just like others in a good and bad world. The world won't always be this way.

Some prophecies from the Bible about the Jews you might enjoy reading:

Amos 9:14-15 written about 750 BC

I will restore my people Israel. They will rebuild the ruined cities and live in them. They will plant vineyards and drink the wine from them. They will plant gardens and eat their fruit. I will plant the people of Israel in their land, and they won't be uprooted again from the land that I gave them, says the Lord your God.

Ezekiel 34:13 written around 590 BC

I will bring them out from the nations, gather them from the countries, and bring them to their own land. I will take care of them on the mountains of Israel, by the streams and the inhabited places of land.

Jeremiah 34:13 written around 620 BC

Hear the word of the Lord, you nations listen to the word of the Lord. Tell it to the distant islands. Say, the one who scattered the people of Israel will gather them and watch over them as a shepherd watches over His flock. The Lord will free the descendants of Jacob and reclaim them from those who are stronger than they are.

Leviticus 26:11-12

I will put my tent among you, and I will never look at you with disgust. So I will live among you and be your God, and you will be my people.

So, whether a person believes in God or not, these prophecies from thousands of years ago have come true about Israel. Israel is the proof.

I'm writing this book at a time when each day there seems to be more and more problems. It is June 26, 2020, and we have corona virus everywhere. We also have people tearing down statues or historical monuments. They try to destroy anything they don't like. Does it eventually get to people they don't like, so they destroy them? I guess they want things to be their way. People have always been the problem on this earth. I've always tried to be optimistic about things. It is not easy to be that way anymore. For one thing we can't pay our debt we owe in the country. It goes up by the trillions so fast; I don't know what it is now. Our messed-up government seems to not pay attention to it, so they don't put it out there for us to see. The bigger problem is the division and hate. The media and our government have so much hate; the country doesn't function like it should. Years and years ago the government tried to work together for the American people. It seems they work mostly for themselves now, and what they want. There are plenty of people outside of the government that are mean and hateful people. They all like to use words like racist if you don't agree with them. A family, a city, or a nation doesn't work together like this. In this world now we should remember what Jesus said. He said to love God and to love one another. If you were to say something like that to these protesters on our streets today, you would be lucky to get away alive. God created all people, and kings, queens, rich and poor are all the same created by Him. The country seems to be headed downward quickly.

I know most people in this world don't consider God, but He would say the problems are because of sin in the world. God and His Son Jesus talked about love and it must be an important thing. It saves people, cities, nations, and the world. We have Satan who pushes lies, and hate, and then we have God who pushes truth and love. We have to pray for this country, and the world. I believe if America fails, so does the world.

The Bible lets us know that we will fail. It is sad, but we are also told that God will not fail. God had a plan, and He still does so eventually we will have a perfect world, just the way He created it long ago.

Since we are born into this creation, and the Bible has been around for a thousand years or more, people don't think of God much. If creation happened last week, or a month ago we would still be talking about it for sure. We would also be praising God for it. We have so many things now; made by God and made by man we have easier lives. Why should we think of God, with such easy lives already? He wants us to. He loves us and is the Creator. He gave us freedom because it was the right thing to do. God didn't want robots that had to love Him. God doesn't create anything that has to love Him.

God didn't create, in the beginning a perfect world all for man and woman where we would all eventually die. God does not make mistakes, but we did. Man and woman, with the tempting from Satan sinned against God, and brought sorrow and death into the world. God warned them.

God wants us to be with Him for eternity. That is His wish, and He is God, so it will be fulfilled. God does not allow sin, so sinful man will not be invited to join Him. Like I said before God being God is all- powerful and can fix the problem, and He did. It was a serious problem. If you can imagine God the Father, God the Son, and God the Holy Spirit having joy together in heaven, well God told His Son He was sending Him on a mission. I have no doubt God's Son knew He would go, but His Father God sent Him. It is just amazing, and was a thing about that word again, love. It was prophesized lots of times in the Bible that Jesus would come, and He would be born miraculously from a virgin young woman. Most of us have heard of Jesus but think about what He did for mankind. Well, He did His Father God's will. He was eventually hit on; spit on, beat up and whipped half to death, taking our punishment for sin. The Son of God, Jesus being God also had power to take everyone's sin. These beatings were not enough so they crucified Him. He died. Jesus did all of this willingly, for one thing it was His Father's will. Being that He was man and God, He felt all the pain and humiliation as a man and God. It was one sacrifice for all mankind. His Father God raised Him to life again, and His Father was very pleased with Him. If you think of what happened God through His Son Jesus made us a way to be with God as sinless people. If we believe Jesus did this for us, we can follow Him back to the Father God. Like creation, this is a kind of power and I should say love, God has for us. God does things, the way they have to be done. Everything about it is mysterious, but the truth is, in the story. God, predicted this in the Bible many times so, who predicts the future, or makes things happen? God does.

There is nothing that we can do to gain salvation in our life. It is a free gift from God. All we can do is believe, and trust in Him. You can't do anything to be saved, except to believe. I'm sure people wonder how we can be sure. You feel it. There is so much proof of God out there, but most people don't take the time to look for it!

Compare what God says about creation, and compare what man says about creation. What scientists and professors say about creation, being that they really don't know, can't know, and they say they don't really know. They do give us their ideas and they are stupid. That is my feeling, but the "big bang" from empty space, soupy pools where life started, then millions of years later evolution ape to man. Most of this stuff sticks, and is partly, if not all, taught in schools. Shame again.

Creation is so huge, well it is just amazing, way beyond us. No part of it can we reproduce. People mostly again just take it all for granted. We have to since we can't explain it. I like to think of a seed, you plant it, and it grows. Everything is set up for human life, perfectly. If you plant a carrot seed, you get a carrot plant and carrots, and the same with all the rest of seeds. Why don't people look at it all?

What about the Bible that God gave us? I've heard it is written by men. We also hear the Holy Spirit was with these writers of the Bible. The Bible should be studied. Scientists and professors should study it. We all should. Why? How about the one God, that created us humans, says it is His Word to us. We can just say we don't believe so why bother. Is there anything like it in the world? It tells us about the beginning of creation, and life, why we have problems, and a story of people, and God. God that has all power, and all knowledge. God that could have willed all creation to happen in a second. He created for us, and brought time into it for us, so He created some each day, through six days, and the seventh day He rested. God doesn't need rest, so He just rested from creation, He was done.

Speaking of time, He allowed people to live long periods of time in the beginning, to populate the earth. How much time do we have? It seems to go slow, and then to go fast. You could say in God's world there is no time. Can you think of what God does without time? He hears thousands to millions, of prayers at the same time, and distinguishes each one. He never dies of course, and walls don't stop Him. Jesus after His resurrection appeared to His disciples, and He didn't come in the door. I write this, because to think of God is interesting. He wants us to think about Him. The thing is most people on this planet don't. No, they don't think about God the Creator, or creation. How about all the varieties of fruit, all varieties of vegetables, and all the meat. Why are there so many varieties of things to eat? We can add things to do on this planet.

God knew having all knowledge, He would have to impress us humans, or we would be lost to Him. This book is about God wanting to get your attention. Do you think God is trying? I was surprised in writing this book, since I wanted, and prayed God might help this country. Now I begin to see what God is doing and has done. He has many helping Him. You need to know, God could, but He is not going to get right in your face and tell you He is God. For one thing, there wouldn't be anyone saying, I don't believe you. God knows how to make people believe. I know in our humanness we can't handle that kind of encounter with God.

I talk this way because most people need a jolt, to find God. They are not looking. Predictions or prophecies are proof of God. No one can predict the future, except God. God can also cause His predictions to come true. There are hundreds of prophecies in the Bible. Many of them have already come true.

I was surprised with these prophecies, while researching them for this book. I had no idea there were so many of them, and what some of them say is amazing. Like a little story of things to come, that were predicted hundreds and thousands of years before. I knew there were prophecies in the Bible, but I didn't know what I was going to find. Let's just say I was very surprised.

To me they are proof of God, and proof of the Bible. There is no excuse or trouble looking them up, now with the internet. Like I said before, get a Bible to check them, but the internet will tell you where they are quickly. I said some are long ago, but some about Israel are much more recent. The Jewish people in Israel are God's chosen people, and there are very interesting prophecies about them. You should ask yourself why this little country is paid so much attention to. They are God's chosen people.

People can just not believe in God but these prophecies in the Bible should make anyone wonder. God can do anything He wants. He can see the future, or He can just make something happen at a certain time in the future.

Israel is restored in the land God gave them. The Bible calls it the Promised Land. It was prophesized that they, and their land would flourish. Check it out, they have flourished. They have a mostly green state, trees, flowers and they grow so much, they sell around the world. They are a powerful little country. They have a powerful ally. Christians look at Israel because they are God's chosen people.

Some countries don't want the Jews in Israel. They don't think it belongs to them, and they likely don't like the idea of them being God's chosen people. The state of

Israel was formed in 1948. They were scattered around the world for over 2000 years. God brought them back and God brought them to that Promised Land, many thousands of years before they were scattered. It has always been their land. They will not be scattered again.

So much has happened while I've been writing this book, and the book is about God and how He is thinking about the country and the world. How are we thinking about the country and the world?

It is now July 15, 2020 and we have corona virus and many problems in the world. Some things going on I can hardly believe. What is wrong with some people out there in our government, and I should add the media outlets. Lots of hate, lies, and just bad stuff. I'm writing about this again, because I , like you must wonder what is to happen next. I'm still working although it has slowed down, I think of the good Americans out there. I pray for all of you out there, that are working and taking care of your families. I know we all feel the weight on us, because of what is happening in our country. I know only God can help and we can still have a smile because God is in charge.

I know most people in the world don't believe in God. The world and our country are getting worse and worse. The main problem, we have is the hate and division.

With the huge debt we have of trillions of dollars, we know it can't be paid back. A strong country like the United States could come back from anything, except for hate and division. I don't like writing about depressing stuff, and we all have to work and keep going. I pray for all of you out there, and I'm sorry we have to put up with it.

We are living in a different world now. Not good different, but bad different. It seems that a lot or most people in our government don't seem to care if the country fails. They just want to get their way. Some of these people are just evil. There is plenty of evil out there.

It seems the news media, our schools, especially universities don't teach our children to care to do what is right, and be prepared to work hard, and always better themselves. The news media is political, and lies, and most professors in universities teach our kids to hate, and don't work hard, try to get everything for free.

I don't like to think that God sees all this craziness going on. This country didn't used to be like this. We humans should want to please God. There are some that do please God, but we all sin, and the world will get worse at pleasing God. It is nice that we have a loving and merciful God.

I know a lot of people pray that God would get rid of this corona virus, at least. It is hard to work together, be around each other, hug, shake hands, or just be people. I don't really think God causes any of this, but I don't know.

This book is about God wanting to get your attention. He has been working on trying to get our attention since creation and the first sin. I halfway joke with my family, that I pray that God would get rid of corona virus, and if He needs to get our attention to send asteroids, or giant grasshoppers. At least we could see them and maybe fight back. It is hard for us to function with this invisible scourge going on.

If sin never entered into this world, we would have a perfect world. God created this world perfect. We sinned and messed up the world. To think that the world is going to get worse is not a pleasant thought, but I need to write about it.

This book is titled God for a reason. God is always working and trying to get our attention. The hate and division is going to bring even a powerful country like ours down. The national debt that everyone knows can't be paid back. We're getting ourselves in trouble. How we are getting in trouble, is not putting God first, and then the hate and division. America didn't used to be this way. Even many commercials on TV have changed.

Change in the way that they are vulgar, not moral, and pushing sexual themes. What's next?

We are supposed to love God, and then love one another. I know it is not easy to love everyone. Like I've said there are good people, bad people and all kinds in between. People are the problem on this earth. We have the Bible, and it is the only book that tells us what went on before, and what is going on now. What is going on, God warned us about thousands of years ago, and again it is the sin.

I've mentioned before that those of you out there that want to find out what is in the Bible, can get help now by using the internet. Keep a Bible handy to double check. I can tell you there is some very interesting writing in it, and all those prophecies are proof of God. It is worth it, you will be amazed, I was. I looked up many prophecies and was surprised. Use your imagination and ask what you think it can answer. I did, and asked what God says about HIs prophecies. I was very surprised. I had to write them in this book, but there are more. Whether you believe in God or not. God having all power, and knowledge, He says what you would think God would say. He says His prophecies will come true, He will cause them to happen, and that He is God, and He will do it. All of them up to this date have come true. Only God can predict the future so you might be interested in checking it out. Many prophecies are scattered all through the Bible. I bet a lot of people don't know about prophecies all through the Bible. Man can't predict the future, or make future events happen. Only God can do this, so it is proof of God, and proof of the Bible. Many of these prophecies have happened when Jesus came to this earth, He fulfilled many prophecies. The latest prophecies are mainly about Israel and the Jewish people. If you know the Bible, you know it says God led the Jewish people to the Promised Land. That was thousands of years ago. It was called the Promised Land because God promised them that land. The Jews are also God's chosen people. They were mainly chosen to let the world know about God. They were to be priests, missionaries and prophets, but they mainly failed. They sinned against God to the point where other countries took them over, and many were scattered. One success was Jesus coming to earth, through the Jewish people.

Now we have a fairly new state of Israel. God forgave the Jews, and brought them back home. He is still bringing them back.

So, is there God? Of course! He predicted and plans the future. God has all power and glory, and creation, and we belong to God. He is a loving and merciful God and is still looking to see what you do. Many of you out in this world are going to continue to not acknowledge

God, or the truth of the Bible. God gave man free will, so it is your choice to pursue the Creator, or not.

You know that God given freedom is the same freedom that we, in this country formed a nation. One nation under God, with liberty, and justice for all. The country originally put God first, and America flourished. If you personally put God first, well, see what happens. We all need Him more today than ever.

The Bible tells us about the latter days when God, who is in charge will say that is enough. Then many people will be hiding, and it will be too late to acknowledge the Creator God. God is not going to put up with the sin, forever. It is not in His plans. Sin was never in His plans.

The Bible tells us that God's creation was good, and He was pleased. When He created man and woman that was good, and He was pleased, God gets the glory for that amazing creation. The mystery of Satan showing up after God's creation of man and tempting Eve to go against God's will, well that must have been in the plans.

Some things we may have questions about that the Bible, and we can't answer, is just the way it is. God gave us what He wanted us to know. We are talking about God that has all power, so we hear about faith. I believe God gave us plenty to believe He is real, but God wants us humans to have faith. Faith in all He says, faith that He sent His Son Jesus to die in our place for our sins.

God knew we would need all He could give us for us to believe.

Only God can predict the future, and especially get it all right. Every prophecy in the Bible has or will come true. There are many of these predictions, or prophecies. People that don't believe in God have no answers for these prophecies. They are just amazing and the whole Bible is amazing. I bet most people that don't believe in God, or the Bible, have not checked out the Bible.

The more you look into the Bible, the more you see. For thousands of years we have been born, and the Bible and creation was already here. We humans take it all for granted. Some things you can't take for granted like all the predictions in the Bible. No one can explain where all of creation came from, or how it happened. Why is there so much, like all the creatures, and all the growth, trees, plants and it just goes on? We can't make any of those things, so we have a mystery. At the top of the list is us. People are incredible, our intelligence, and what we can do. There is something more, and most people feel it.

Writing about God, and how He feels about us, of course is not easy. The reason is something you might not expect. The words can never be good enough, when writing about God. Maybe just watching the clouds going by in the blue sky, seeing the wildflowers, and sunsets is enough to at least get started in thinking about God. That is some of the things He Did in creation for us to enjoy.

It is interesting thinking of this invisible God, and all the things that are visible He made. If He didn't, then who did? People like to think of many ideas when it comes to creation and life. Most people don't think of it much at all. We have everything we could ever want and as time goes on, we will have more stuff. There are things in this world we don't need , hate , violence, murder and more. The Bible has different writings on life. Why do we have this, the Bible? The most sold book ever.

We humans have something in us that causes us to want to seek the Creator. Since people mostly take creation for granted, and we have so many conveniences in life that slows us down in seeking the Creator. Why wouldn't man want to seek the Creator? If we think of these human bodies we have, they are amazing. Who designs such a thing? Our bodies and mind? Of all the creatures on this earth, only humans think of our mortality. We hurt and feel awful when our loved ones die, and friends. We know it will soon be our turn. Our relatives that are still here can grieve over us.

Is there anything that explains about life, and death and why? Only the Bible. The Bible should be of interest to us all.

We have to think about people on this world. We have good people, bad people, and certainly all kinds in between. I don't understand many people out there. It seems that a lot of people want to hurt our country. We can figure the people that want to defund, or get rid of the police, are also trying to hurt this country. There are no perfect people on this earth, and it seems that we will all fight for power over one thing or another. Our government is a good example of senseless, wanting of power. It is senseless and there is only one answer to it all, and of course that is God. People can't handle power. They might want more. Satan did. Why do some people want power? Power over other people. I would hope people with power look to God, in using their power. God has all power.

We have dictators ruling over some countries, and they have power and like it. I don't like power that rules over other people. We are getting samples of this in our country. I know we will always have people with powerful positions. They should do what is right and be fair to all others. Well, we get back to having good people, bad people, and all kinds in between. People should all practice do onto others, as you would have them do unto you. Is the country, and the world getting away from that kind of thinking? Well, I figure God created perfectly, there was no sin, and God was around. God was right to give man freedom, or free will, so Satan was allowed to tempt us, and we sinned.

Well now I see we have so called protesters destroying anything they can. They are violent and mean, and should not have the right to hurt others, and the country.

This is still the best country in the world. The God given freedom we have, has made this a great country. I don't know why some want to hurt the country and hurt other people. We have evil people in our country.

We are all sinners in this country, and the world. I and many others in this country remember the word love. I still believe that most people want to help others and help the country to be better. We just seem to be getting more and more people out there and many in our government that are filled with hate. I don't know if they like being like that, or maybe they don't think that they hate. Some people want their own way and won't listen to others. Those that hurt other people, burn down businesses and other things, are full of hate.

Back in the past people came to America and were thrilled to be here . It wasn't easy for these people, but they had freedom. Now people take this freedom for granted. Some use freedom to take advantage of the system. Foreigners that come to America, legal, or illegal take advantage of our freedom. They don't try to become good Americans and blend in like people used to do.

We have problems now in our schools, in our government, and most of our news outlets. The way the country was set up, is now messed up. Remember one nation under God, and in God we trust. Now many in our schools, in our government, in our news outlets run the country down. The country has made mistakes, and that is because people make mistakes. We still have the best country in the world, but because of people, and sin it isn't what it used to be.

America has done so much good for the rest of the world. If some of you out there want to rundown America, why do you get to judge it? Do you want things America is not giving you? It is still mostly a free country, and anyone has a choice to succeed in life. Some of you should probably leave America and go to a country where you can be happy. If you can, let us know where that is.

When hurricanes, earthquakes and tsunamis happen in the world, who goes to help? America! We are capable of helping, so we do. We can't do everything, but we do a lot. What about in past wars we help the losers rebuild and we helped others that were involved. No other country does this ever, rebuilding a country after we help destroy them, because of war. How come they don't teach about the good news of America in our schools? America had the freedom for its people to be able to work hard and make a life for their families. In doing so the people of America made the country a powerful nation. America was not the kind of country, or people to want to bother other countries. We made this country one nation under God and in God we trust. Because of our government America has made past mistakes. All humans do.

Many countries in the past have claimed parts, or all of other countries, in the name of their king, or queen, and sometimes religion.

America, a younger country has always just wanted to protect our God given freedom. There are many in our own country now that wants to chip away at our freedom. Those people should leave America, since they are already many countries that have less freedom, these people can move to.

I could go on and on about the good things America stands for, and good things America does and has done. I write about these things and could write much more about the good of America. Now we have many in our government and many more people all over, that rundown our country. I say shame on them. We should all want to make it better. Some people are just too full of hate.

How about do unto others as you would have them do unto you? I know there are people out there that would just laugh at that statement. Maybe you people should think of God.

The world and our country is going downhill. Humans are the problem, but not all humans. Those humans that are agitators, and hate-filled yell and scream the most and the loudest. I for one don't understand you. You want things, you can't have, and you want more of things you don't deserve, so you want to tear up the country.

There is one thing that is perfect in this world, and that is God. He has all power, and He created us and gave us free will. So, you can act however you want but He is the judge of all of us, not you.

You can use your free will to not believe in God, and if you want to destroy things, burn up things and hurt people, and our country you only help prove God. God is not like you, or any of us and the world, and you belong to God the Creator.

How far does good go in this world? That may sound like a strange question. It is a question worth asking, since we do have good and bad in the world. The good has to go all the way to life, and God. The bad has to go all the way down to death and the devil.

We take the freedom of America a little for granted, and we take creation a lot for granted. We were all born into this creation.

Why do some people work hard for God? This is another question that is worth asking, since we know many people do work for God. Are these people stupid? They usually seem to be caring and intelligent. Do they have a feeling of God? Yes! They have God's spirit in them. It is a mystery also about how close you can be to God, since we live in this good and bad world.

We hear about sin in the Bible a lot. No one on this earth is without sin, even those of us that are close to God, sin. We just live in a messed-up world. All I have to say after saying it is a messed-up world, it is also a beautiful and wondrous world. God made it, but He made it perfect. God's plan is for everything to be perfect again, and that is what He is going to do. God already fixed everything through His Son Jesus, and now He waits for all of us who will come to Him. You know that most people on this earth don't pay attention to creation, God, or the Bible? God is not just waiting for people to come to

Him, through His Son Jesus; He is working on it, and has help.

This is all because God loves you and He wants you to be a part of His family forever. That is amazing to me. God wants to help us. Like I said at the beginning of this book, He is trying to get your attention. God gave us a choice, and so we have the choice to want to be with God or not.

Since people are born into this creation, people will keep taking it for granted.

We humans were created curious, and so we want to learn. Think about our children that ask questions. If they heard of God, they might ask where God came from, or who made God. We should ask ourselves about all these amazing things, and where they came from. Let's quit thinking comets brought life to earth, or aliens. They had to be created. Why not think of God, He certainly thinks of us.

Scientists and professors want us to think the universe, this earth, and us, just happened somehow. I say somehow because they don't know. They even say they are not sure. They want to leave God out. To think we evolved from apes is stupid, and a cold way of thinking. Apes are just the closest thing to what a human looks like. Apes are animals and we humans were never animals. We are amazing because we were created in God's image.

If we could get back to us humans taking everything for granted, if God took away our taking everything for granted, we would be amazed. We were just born into this creation. Most people don't think about the earth moving around the sun at approximately 67,000 miles per hour. We enjoy the beautiful sunsets, the clouds moving across the blue sky, and the wildflowers. Since there are people that wonder about all of this, and we had no answers, God gave us the Bible. God knew we needed answers, so He gave us what He wanted us to know. Most people on this earth don't believe in the Bible, or God. If you study the Bible, you would be surprised. You would see truth about life, and many predictions of things that have happened, and things to come.

With over seven billion people on this earth, only a fraction of them believe in God and the Bible. Just the prophecies in the Bible are proof of God. Only God can predict future events. Problems in our country and the world are happening at a faster pace. People that don't know this aren't paying attention, and likely take creation and all for granted.

Like I said before we have a better way of checking out prophecies in the Bible. Find them on the internet and look them up in the Bible. You will be surprised, I was. There are so many that describe things only God could know.

Many archaeological finds around Israel and the Middle East, have also proven the Bible correct.

I think of the scientist, I read about in the past that tried to prove the Bible wrong. He used his knowledge and investigated it, and finally he became a Christian. He couldn't prove it wrong, and he probably noticed all the predictions, by God in the Bible and couldn't prove them wrong.

You might not understand everything in the Bible, but that doesn't mean it's not true. We also can't understand an all-powerful God.

I've talked to a person about the Bible story of Jonah. God wanted Jonah to do something and Jonah didn't want to do it. Well Jonah ended up in the belly of a great fish. Our thinking tells us a person couldn't live long in the belly of a fish. He was there three days. He decided to do what God wanted him to do. If God can make a man out of dirt, and breathe the breath of life into him, and bring life to him, He can make Jonah uncomfortable in a giant fish for three days and stay alive.

What do you think God wanted Jonah to do for Him? In past times God used prophets and others like Jonah, Moses, and others to deliver messages to people. The message has never changed, so what does God want us to do? Same as what He wanted back then. God doesn't change and is consistent. He wants us to acknowledge that He alone is God, and the Creator of everything. He also wants us to love Him since He loves us. He also wants us not to sin. Think about what God wants is for us to be a part of His family for eternity. You would think humans would want that, but most of us take creation for granted, and don't even acknowledge God.

God wants humans to be with Him and you have to go through Jesus, the Son of God to get there.

Why is it not so easy to talk to other people about Jesus? Maybe because you are trying to change their life, or is it to save their life? We are all different, and God uses people in different ways. How, and why God uses people to help Him, is we have to first think of all the people we see out there, that are not paying attention. They don't think of God or very little. If people just live in the world, well, the world is going to go downward, and we are too. How can we walk on this amazing earth, and not think of God? Well, that is the way it is, on a good, and bad world.

Humans were created with an inner spirit to seek the Creator. That Creator seeks us, but He gave us a choice. How nice and perfect was that to give us a choice. The only thing we have to know is in time God is going to make everything back to loving, and perfect again. That is the way He is, and that is what He will do. Everything God has said, or says, He will accomplish. That's the way He is. He is wonderful and has all power. We should all want to be with Him, and He wants us to be.

This book I am writing certainly causes me to think about God a lot. I also think a lot about God 's creation. I think also about us humans and God. God created everything for us humans, but it all belongs to Him. We belong to Him.

The Bible tells us a lot about God and ourselves and many more things. The Bible says God loves us all. God is not like us He loves everyone the same. Like I said before, God just hates sin not the person.

This kind of thinking on God's part should make everyone in our country think about the pushing of racism in the country. God would say people are being ridiculous, and I say the same. God doesn't care if you are a prince, if you're rich, He created us all, and we are all the same. We are humans. Color of skin doesn't matter; we are all human, and the same.

You know that people come down on Christianity, and God likely because The Bible talks about the high standard of perfection God sets for us. Don't be too concerned about it since none of us measure up. Not a person on the planet measures up. That is where our most wonderful savior comes in, Jesus, His Father God sent Jesus to fix the problem of sin and He did. It had to be done like it was. It was very extreme, but Jesus had to fix it. Think that after it was done, it is called a free gift to us all.

If we think back to the first sin, which caused the downfall of this earth, and death we need to think of the wonderful, and perfect world God created. It was also perfect that God created man and woman and gave them freedom or free will. Adam and Eve didn't know what sin was until Satan tempted Eve to sin, and Eve tempted Adam. It may seem like God allowed Satan to tempt Eve. God created perfect and gave Adam and Eve free will. God told Adam and Eve not to eat of the tree of the knowledge of good and evil. If they did, they would surely die. It is mysterious, but we have come a long way since that first sin. This sin is easy to believe, we can only look at the world today. With the over seven billion people on this earth, we have lots of sin since no one is without sin.

It all happened because God created us, and He wanted us to be with Him for eternity. This is not something we can understand, at least not now. It all gets back to that word love. God created us in His image and loves us. If all of this is gone someday, there will still be God. There will also be lots of people with God. Do all of these believers in God, and His Son Jesus, and the Holy Spirit just have a feeling for God? Yes! You don't have to see God like the wind, you feel God. Is there proof of God? Yes! Unimaginable creation proves God. The Bible and all the prophecies in the Bible prove God. You should know people prove God. Something much better than us, made us. Man was created intelligent. God has all knowledge and power.

It is the bad in this world that makes us not think of God, who is the good in the world.

The technology in this world which moves faster than we can keep up with, it is also good, and bad. If we think God gave us the intelligence to understand, and make new things, we use the resources that are in the ground mostly to do it. Everything we use comes from God. We came from God, and people have to realize that humans are amazing. So are all the other creatures, and plant life on earth. Why is it that with all the intelligence, understanding, and skill of humans, the majority of people don't give credit to a Creator? Partly because we have all we need and want for a good life. We have pain, sickness, and death. Day by day we get older, at least these bodies get weak, not the spirit. What is going on? God tells us what is going on in His Word, the Bible.

We all go through times where we just live our lives our own way. God gave us that freedom. Is living our lives our own way ok in the big scheme of things? When we are strong and healthy, we don't think about it much. We all just go through a short time, when we are strong and healthy. Some people don't even get that. We don't understand why children are inflicted with disease, and others. I believe it gets back to the bad and good world we live on. It is still interesting because there is so much beauty and goodness on this earth. It is getting worse, and people are the cause. Love and the beauty will win in the end. I don't know how long it will be, but God does. God created everything perfectly and eventually He is going to get His way. He fixes things like when He sent His Son Jesus. It has been over 2000 years since Jesus came. Jesus came to do His Father's will. Since sin brings death, Jesus being God the Son, didn't sin, but took all sin on Himself and died with it. He did this willingly for us, and because His Father God willed Him to do it. Jesus was brought back to life by His Father God. The Bible, or God's Word, tells us we can follow Jesus through death, through the grave and right into the arms of God. God wants us, to live for eternity with Him. Now God is waiting but working with many people to get everyone's attention. It is not going that well since most people are not thinking of creation. Man keeps creating things like iPads, computers, and more to keep people occupied. Like I've said before, these things are not bad, depending on what you do with them. Try texting God. Look up some of God's prophecies from the Bible. You will be surprised if you do. I was, and I'm still thinking about them. Only God can predict or make things happen. He has, and He keeps on doing it.

God wants us to know that He gave us the Bible. It is called the Holy Bible, because God is Holy, and the Bible is inspired by the Holy Spirit. Men may have written the Bible, but God protected it, and always has.

I've thought of that word glory and only God deserves glory. In His perfect creation, God got the glory, and you could say He lost part of it through Satan, and angels, and us, we all sinned. We caused sin in God's perfect world. God is going to get all the glory because He fixed things through His Son Jesus. Jesus, the Bible says was glorified, when He was brought back to life, by His Father God. Every human that comes to God, and believes, God gets glory. God's will is going to be done. God, we just don't understand really well. For instance, if you sin a lot, you can go to God for help. Yes, He is against sin and hates it, but He loves you. If you want His help, He wants to help. Only He can. It is truly an amazing thing; God has done for us. He gave us a free gift of His Son Jesus that sits to the side of His Father God, in heaven. Jesus intervenes for us believers on this earth because we are not perfect. We know we need Jesus to help us and He does. We try but we sometimes sin, and are not happy about it. Jesus already paid the price for our sin. Amazing.

It is how hard can we try not to sin, after what Jesus did for us.

That is where the Holy Spirit comes in. The Holy Spirit miraculously lives in believers to help them, and do stuff like help in writing this book, and think of Jesus more. Wow!

Do you look at the beauty in creation, and think that God made these magnificent things for you? The leaves hanging from the trees, the twigs, and the birds. God created them by saying it so. People take things for granted, like I've said before. Do we need more miracles to believe? We have miracles all the time on this planet and take them for granted also. A seed that grows into a plant of any kind is a miracle. Babies that are born are miracles. Human babies the Bible says God breathes the breath of life into them.

We all want God to do something for us, like when a loved one is sick and dying. We don't understand why people die young, or get injured, and God having all power could heal them. When sin came into the world, people started dying then. We should pray for people but, we are all going to die. God's creation had nothing to do with death, only life. God is not responsible for death. God warned Adam and Eve in the garden of Eden, not to eat the fruit from one tree. The tree of the knowledge of good and evil. God told them they would surely die if they ate fruit from that tree. So, Satan tempted Eve to eat the fruit and she did. Things were perfect before that. There was no sin in the world before eating the fruit, God told them not to do it.

I'm sure we all have several questions about this story of eating the fruit, and sin entering the world. I think being that God gave man freedom, or free will we were bound to sin. It is just a mystery.

Many of us know what the Bible tells us about the early time after creation, when there was no Bible, God was more involved. God still worked in people's lives and tried to get them to do what was right. God had a few that were close to Him called prophets. They took word from God to people of what God wanted them to know. With the sin in the world, like today, God was forced to deal with sinful men. Back then in that part of the world some people worshipped idols. Like Egypt that had all kinds of Gods, they worshipped, and it went into other countries. Even God's chosen people the Hebrew (Jews), some worshipped idols. God would certainly get angry about that. God did many things for those people, and through time they would not pay attention to this, invisible God and start worshipping something they could see. It still goes on. People worship other things, and not God. There came a time when people were so far into sin that God considered doing away with His creation, man. We had the great flood, and there were only a few that God spared. A few that were close to God. Most of us know the story of the flood. Some people of course don't believe in the flood. We know you can find pieces of shark's teeth in desert areas. I know there are questions about this flood, and other things the Bible tells us about. Some people since they don't understand they also don't believe. God that created everything we see, and has all power and knowledge, we can't imagine that either.

When God gave us the Bible the history of civilization was part of it. It talked about the time before people had the Bible, and before the time of Jesus. You can read about it in the Bible.

Something some of us might think about is, when God caused bad people to die, and there were innocent babies that would have died with them, isn't that sinful? It is interesting thinking of these things. It is part of what we don't understand. I believe God as Creator can get rid of part or all of this creation if He wants to. There would be no sin involved, God wants a perfect world like He originally created, He will eventually have what He wants. Most of us just don't try to understand God. What He created, us, He loves. He created us perfect.

The innocent babies I mentioned that would have died in the flood, or any other time, might have gone straight to heaven. Only God knows, but we know God is fair and just. We as humans, if we think about God, and He wants us to, we really understand very little. This is exactly why God sent His Son Jesus and made sure we have the Bible. The Bible says God is a God of love. God says He loves every one of us.

Because of not looking to God, and just doing what the world offers, most people don't know and don't believe in God. That would also mean that humans are the best, and brightest on the planet. Well we are the destroyers, by our attitude, and the lack of love. There has to be something more and there is, and always has been, and always will be. That is God, who is continuing to try to get your attention.

When God sent His Son, Jesus, to do His mission on this earth, it was for us. Jesus conquered sin and death, and gave us the way to His Father God. It is all written in God's Word, the Bible. God is going to make things like He intended them to be when He first created, without sin. Eventually sin and death will be no more, and pain and sorrow will be gone. Jesus said He is the way, the Truth, and the Life and no man goes to the Father except through Him.

Like the prophecies in the Bible, God is going to accomplish what He says. Many people on this earth are not going to follow Jesus or look for God. God waits and works because He wants as many that will to be a part of His family. That is why God created, but Satan and man and woman threw a wrench into creation with sin. Most people don't think about this, but you can see how the world is a mixture of good and bad. The world and our country are gradually getting worse.

The Bible is the only book and only place where you can read about good and bad, life and death, and history back to the beginning of man. The only alternative we can believe is ape to man. Man evolving from an ape like creature is a cold way of thinking. Humans are so special that only a supreme being, God, could have made us. Just our eyes alone I've read there are thousands of nerve connections in a square inch. Did our eyes evolve, and our fingers and toes? No! Man and woman were created by God perfectly, and had a language and intelligence, and talked to God.

Many people on this planet put down Christianity and God. Why? They have the freedom to do that, and they also want to do what they want. We know we have a planet of people that think many different things concerning God. Some countries are communist, and frown on people that believe in God. You can even get in trouble in those countries if you are known to believe in God! In America, and other countries you are free to believe, or worship God however you like. Mostly people don't think about it much. That is just my opinion. It gets back to why I am writing this book. So many people take creation and the Bible for granted. If God created everything, and the Bible is true, then it should be important for people to check it out. We are all born into this creation and the Bible has been around for hundreds of years so people don't pay attention.

There is so much in the world to do, computers, TV, travelling and just unlimited things to do. Probably ninety-nine percent of things we can do on this planet, God gave us, and they are not sinful. We still have a big problem; we all know about, we will eventually all die. Only one place gives us information about life and death, and that is the Bible. Some people might want to argue about the Bible being true, or not. The thing is the Bible can't be proven wrong. What about the prophecies or predictions by God scattered all through the Bible?

Like I said, look on the internet and find prophecies, and look them up in the Bible. You will be surprised. I was. Ask the computer what God says about His prophecies? You will be really surprised. God says, many things and He says these predictions of things that have happened, and things that will happen. Only He will make them happen. Only God can see the future, or cause things to happen in the future. All the history in the Bible, and the things not talked about anywhere else, and all the prophecies that all have happened and will happen prove God, and the Holy Word the Bible.

When standing up for God and the Bible you have to wonder why so many people take it all for granted. I have to bring up someone, or something that is called Satan, again. For some reason he is around to work in people's minds. Satan does not want you to believe in God. He also wants you to do evil, which gets you away from God. Of course, many people do bad things, and evil, without Satan's help. You have to acknowledge good and bad in the world, even if you don't believe in God or Satan. It looks like the bad is getting worse.

Why do people want their way, even when they are wrong? Like the protestors that hurt other people, and destroy property. These kinds of people are not easy to understand, because they seem to enjoy violence, and destruction.

China is causing lots of trouble in the world. I should say the Chinese Communist government. Not the Chinese people. How about the American government, maybe a lot of them are taking lessons from the Chinese government? Like the Chinese government, that would like to rule the world, we have people in our government, and protestors that want power and want their way. Shame on all of you. What is the deal about being above others, using the racist word to help get your way? Most of us Americans don't understand people like you. Do you know the phrase, "Do unto others, as you would have them do unto you"? How about live and let live? You hurt the county and the world, wanting your way. I know you can't say anything to these kinds of people. We should pray for them, since that is about all we can do. They are just mean, violent, and destructive people. We have many in our country like them.

With bad and good in the world, and I am talking about people, of course. We are the creatures on earth with a choice to try to do good, or bad. It is people that mess things up. The Bible explains it well, it is called sin. If bad is sin, then what is good? Love. Well, we have to much hate in the world.

What I've been writing about, hate and sin will bring the country down, and the world. I don't like writing about it, and I know you don't like reading about it, and that is sin. Only God can help. All people sin in some way, even in our thoughts. God sees sin as sin, course some sin is worse than other sin.

With stuff going on that is bad, and going to only get worse, is there a way to be happy? Yes! There is a calling out there, and it comes from God's Son Jesus. He alone gave us a reason to be happy. Jesus is with His Father God in heaven, and they have great joy together. We can have joy by knowing we can be a part of that family. We don't understand this mighty God, since He says they are a three in one God. We talk about God, we talk about Jesus, and we talk about the Holy Spirit. God has been this kind of God forever. If you think of this trinity God, as humans we don't' understand, we just believe it because God says it is so. There is much more we can't understand since we are talking about a God that has all- power, and knowledge. How about being everywhere at one time or hearing millions of prayers at the same time, and knowing each one. God lives outside of time. Time is for us humans.

We were created for some reason. Do you think God was lonely? No! God the Father doesn't get lonely, and especially with a Son like Jesus with Him. They have great joy together and add God the Holy Spirit. If I say they when I write about the trinity, it is ok, but we don't need to talk that way. It is interesting and, in my writing, saying they, or three in one. I do pray God understands. Well I barely understand, but I'm writing about this and all I can say is, we have a mighty God. The thing is that when we pray, we usually pray to the Father God, as one God. We can pray or talk to Jesus in our prayers and we can thank the Great Helper the Holy Spirit. They are all the truth and they are one God.

If God the Trinity was not lonely why did He create us, and angels also? He created us and gave us free will, to do as we wanted. Well He did and we sinned, against what God wanted. It seems like we were an experiment. All we know is what God lets us know in the Bible. God wants us to live with Him for eternity. That is very nice of God, after how we act on this earth. I know most people don't think about what God has done for us. What He has done for us goes on and on. If we could take away all the bad stuff and sin on this planet that Satan and we are responsible for we would have a perfect world. There would be no death or sorrow. That is the way God created it, and He will have it that way again.

Some people may think some sin is fun to do. Since we grew up on this earth with sin, that might be partly true. Then you should think if we grew up near God, what would He have for us to do? That is interesting since we are talking about God who has all power and knowledge.

God has created other things like angels. He gave them free will like us, but they are not like us. They have power. Angels are with God, so they know God, but it didn't stop one angel, Lucifer from going against God. He was jealous of God, and wanted power like God. Lucifer convinced maybe a third of the other angels to go with him when he was kicked out of heaven. We don't understand all of this. Lucifer has many names now. He is called Satan and the devil.

Most of, if not all of life, and creation is a mystery. The smartest people on earth don't have the answers. The smartest people will usually agree with things like man evolved from ape, and the "big bang" in empty space. Like I said before, that is cold thinking. If God is left, out of a person's thinking you really can't even figure correctly. If you figure all the prophecies in the Bible, and the archeological finds, and just a lot of plain wisdom in the Bible, you need to add God into the mystery of creation and life. Think also of God's chosen people, the Hebrews (Jewish) people. God is bringing them back from being scattered all over the world. God also blessed them, and their little country just flourishes, even though they are surrounded by Arab countries that don't really like them.

If God, heaven, and Satan is a mystery to people and we disregard them we still have a mystery. We still have creation that was designed for us humans. I believe it is our calling to investigate this mystery. How about all the varieties of food on this planet? It was all set up for us. Everything was intended for us humans.

If I could just write about God, that would be a happy thing. I know God wants me to write about the unhappiness also. To be with God, gives happiness. To only live in this world without God it is not so happy. We just live on an imperfect world.

Perfect in what God created, but not perfect in the sin. We all have ups and downs on this earth, so if we strive to be close to God it makes things smoother. That is what He wants us to do. There is happiness with family, and other things, and friends can make us happy. We all still have an underlying problem in our country and the world. It is division, hate, and just evil.

Since I've been writing this book, you could say I'm writing about God and all that is wrong at the right time. It seems like we keep getting more and more problems in our country. I've mentioned problems and then come more problems.

We have people in the country and the world that wants God put to the side or taken out of things. It started years ago, like in our schools and more. We can't push God around, but people can stay farther away from Him.

That is certainly happening. If you are bothered by what is going on in our country, there is only one place for help and that is God. You might also wonder why God doesn't do something to help the country. I prayed and wished He would. God works in different ways, and He wants to see what we are going to do. Many people are doing different things to help. It seems like it isn't enough. I'm writing this book and never figured on doing it. I wished and prayed that God would somehow help our children and grownups that move around on this earth taking everything for granted. Like creation, the Bible, and God. Since you can't see God, most people don't think about Him. Most people just stay busy doing one thing or another and don't think about creation, life, and God. We all have times in our life that we don't think much about those things. I did, I believed, but I spent my life the way I wanted. God wants us to live our life a different way, close to Him. God having all power and knowledge He certainly knows the best thing for us, better than we do.

So, we get back to God is working to get your attention, and people are helping Him. Remember when Jesus came, He also was here on this earth working to help people understand and seek God. He gave His life for this reason and His Father God willed Him to do it. Remember since the wages for sin is death, that is why

Jesus took sin on Himself and died in our place. Jesus was perfect and the Son of God, so He accomplished what His Father God wanted Him to do. His Father God brought Jesus back to life and was certainly pleased with Him. Why did God do all of this for us? He created us perfectly, and He loves us. He will get everything back to the perfect creation, before sin.

How can people believe in all of this? Is it just faith? Proof of this invisible God is everywhere. We are just living our lives on this planet that was perfectly created for that.

Why do we have good and bad in this world? We seem to get used to it. Only the Bible explains about it. Most things you can enjoy doing on this planet are good things, but there is a lot of bad. We can see it.

Why are humans the only ones on this planet that figure, and plan, and we can think about our mortality. Like I've written about before, we are all going to die. I don't like writing about sadness but look at our world that is getting worse. Will we all be around in 200 years, or even 50 years? I kind of doubt it, or maybe much fewer of us. It is most likely that humans will do ourselves in, one way or another.

God's Word says He didn't create us to die. God doesn't create for death, but for life. That is why after we sinned,

God had to fix it through His Son Jesus. It is amazing that Jesus took sin on Himself, and died taking it from us humans! Only God could do that, and Jesus is God the Son.

Creation in the beginning was perfect, and man was perfect. With Satan's help man sinned, which caused all the problems. It caused an imperfect world. God loves us so He did something else perfect. He sent His Son Jesus to fix the sin problem. So, you think God the Father, God the Son, and God the Holy Spirit, should be praised for this? Being that Jesus lived here on this earth, He felt the beatings, being spit on, whipping, and the dying of His own free will, for us. Jesus can't die, but He did willingly to save us and it was the will of His Father God. It was a big price to pay to save us from sin, and it was a perfect plan. Most people on this earth don't believe in all of this. Think if it is true we can't pay God back for all of this. God says it is a free gift. We only have to accept it. Do you think if God did all of this for us, should we give Him some of our time? Some people just give God maybe an hour on Sunday. I'm not running anyone down because we are all sometimes neglecting God. We should just let God know we love Him and thank Him for what He has done for us. God wants you to humble yourself, and talk to Him. If you think of the over seven billion people on this planet, only a small percentage talks to God. If you would say God doesn't talk back, I would say He certainly hears. He has His own way, so keep alert. We don't need the Creator talking to us audibly. It would likely be hard to handle. He doesn't try to be secret, or mysterious. He is not human, and He works different than us for sure. If you pursue God, He will pursue you in ways that are not that explainable. You might get a feeling, or feelings you haven't had before. Some might say it is just all in our mind. That is true, in our mind, and our total being.

I know on this planet with the good and bad, God does things with people who believe and love Him. You need to be aware of them. God doesn't do bad things of course, so all the good things that happen, are they just coincidences? If you love God, I don't think they are coincidences. I know we will still have bad things happen because that is the way it is on this planet. God I believe likes to do small things, just to see if we notice, or if we are paying attention. We as humans want God to do what we would think of as a big thing, like healing a loved one. The earth was set in motion, and has sin and death. God can do anything, and why He doesn't do what we would like, we can't answer. God doesn't cause pain, and death. We caused pain, and death with the help from Satan. There is a mystery, but the Bible explains it pretty well.

The interesting little things God does, I think He enjoys doing them because He can. Also, I believe He wants to let you know He is around, or even like a hello. If you believe, you should also pay attention. Like you hear God works in mysterious ways. You could say that everything good that happens, that might be even a little odd, is just a coincidence. We think God has to do big things. God is different and God doesn't think like us humans. He loves us and certainly cares so why wouldn't He put little good or interesting things in our lives to make us wonder. I wish I had written down all the little things God does. I just don't call all of the thing's coincidences. Like I've said we have bad things happen to us in this world. You could make a big list, like flat tires, washing machine quits, and more. We have to believe on our own, and this invisible God is not going to do great miracles, and make us believe in Him. He doesn't want robots that have to believe in Him, or love Him, so I believe He likes to do little things to see if we notice. That is my opinion, since I do know He wants to get your attention. These little things I think He does, is going to be a little different. I don't think these things happen that often, but I think they happen. I believe so why wouldn't they happen? God is not just sitting on His throne doing nothing. If you love God, I think He will be in touch with you. He just works in different ways than we humans might think.

Is God going to make everything better? While we live on this good and bad world the only thing that gets better is being close to God. When Jesus came to this planet the Jewish people thought the Messiah was going to come and make their lives just great. They figured some prophecy suggested that. They didn't recognize Jesus as the Son of God. He performed miracles, but He didn't make all their lives better. They were ruled by the Romans at the time. Jesus did just what was needed and what His Father God wanted Him to do. He taught about God in heaven, and didn't try to take credit for anything. He gave all credit to the Father God in heaven. The people of that day didn't realize Jesus was to take the sin of the world on Himself and die in our place. So, Jesus made things all better and most of the people then didn't know. Many of the religious leaders back then didn't understand Jesus, and even wanted Him killed. They got their wish. I'm sure they were surprised when Jesus dying on the cross said "Father forgive them, for they know not what they do ".

Since the time of the first sin, God has been trying to get our attention. People are all born into this creation, and the Bible has been around for hundreds of years. People now take all of it for granted, and they move about this planet doing their own thing. So, God wants to get your attention. He does have a following of believers, which try to help. When Jesus was on this planet, He was doing His Father's will, trying to get people's attention. So back to why God wants to get people's attention. He created everything and us. Everything belongs to God, and He loves us. We were created in His image. God wants us to know, if people just take everything for granted, and don't use the freedom or free will God gave us, and turn to Him; eventually we will lose the chance to be with God. If you believe man evolved from ape and the world and universe just popped up somehow, you won't be a part of God's world. God gave us a choice, and gave us the Bible to help us understand

Is there not enough proof of God so people don't believe, or do they just not think about it? Both reasons are true, and people are all different, and think all different ways. If you investigate a little, there is proof of God. He gave it to us. In my writing this book, I've become amazed in doing some investigating of God. People can just not believe and live their life the way they want, and not try to find out about the mystery of life. The Bible says seek and you will find, knock and the door will be opened. A lot of people don't start seeking any answers until they get older and soon, they will die. Some never get the chance because they die. We are all good at putting certain things off. Trying to figure out life is something we put off. God continues His work since He does not want to lose you. Think of it this way, if you die without God in your life you stay without God in your life. I'll also say God is fair and that is God's business. He sees in people's heart. Some say what matters when you are dead. That is not what the Bible says. Only the outer covering dies like a tent. Our inner being or spirit, that doesn't age is going to be with God, or without God.

What are some proofs of God? Creation, and just so much of it. Humans are so amazing, all having different fingerprints, different eyes, we can figure and do so many things, and think of a Supreme Being or God. We also know of our mortality. No other creature is like that. The Bible gives proof of God. It tells us things you can't get anywhere else. It has prophecies all through the Bible. For unbelievers prophecies are a problem. No one can tell us what will happen in the future, but God can. He not only tells of future events, but He also causes them to happen. Many of these prophecies have happened, and some we are waiting for. God says they will come true. Some prophecies were prophesized hundreds of years before they happened, and some thousands.

It is easy to check out prophecies now, using a computer. Keep a Bible handy look them up, and punch in prophecies from the Bible. You will get more than you'll want to look up.

I was surprised when I looked up, what does God say about these prophecies? God says plenty, that the prophecies will all happen, and He will do it. Some prophecies happened long ago, like many prophecies of the coming of Jesus. Prophecies of God's chosen people and Israel are much more recent. Long ago it was predicted that Jewish people would be scattered all over the world. You'll see it also predicted God would gather them up again, and bring them back to their Promised Land, Israel, that God gave them.

The Jews were scattered over 2000 years ago. There wasn't even a country when they started coming back. There was swampy land, desert, and maybe a few mud shacks. God is with them, and they won't be scattered again. They became the state of Israel in 1948.

While writing this book the world has gotten another problem, corona virus. It has been going on for a couple of months now. It saddens me to think of what it is doing to our country. I pray for all people and the country. It seems like things keep happening like violent protests, problems with police. Is there any love out there, or is it hate and division? I know there is love, but it must be fading some.

China wants to take over the world. Their government not the people. I don't know why people want power like that. How about the American government? Three words sum it up hate, division, and lies. Shame on them. Many people in our country are like the government.

With the huge debt our country has, and no possibility of paying it back, what is going to happen? Nothing good can happen when you have so much division and hate.

Before I ever heard of the corona virus, I was writing this book about God. I know God wanted me to write this, and why wouldn't He? I'm not anyone special so I wondered a little about why I'm doing this. I believe God is helping me, since we are all sinners on this planet, maybe I care about people. I don't want to bring attention to myself, but I want to bring attention to God. What I know is God has been trying to get our attention, since He created us.

Some people might wonder if God caused the corona virus. We would deserve whatever the Creator wanted to do. Look at the millions of abortions, the hate, and so much more. We have a God of love, He created us, and set up the universe for life on planet earth. God does not want to hurt us, He wants to help us. We don't know that what happens to us on this earth may be God's will to get our attention. Has anything God has done, like creation, like giving us the Bible helped to get our attention? Many people it has helped. People just walk the earth and take everything for granted. You see the beauty God made. We see the fluffy clouds float by in the blue sky, and so much more. Many people think creation just happened, or it came about in ways that make no sense.

People like I said before, have always had trouble with an invisible God. Everything on this planet, that is good has God's name on it. It all belongs to God, and so do we. People were given the freedom by God to want to belong to God, or not belong to Him.

We are weak and He is strong, and He could make the corona virus gone in a second. What God does is always good, and He is the Creator. He easily has power to make everything, good for us, but is it His will? God is not going to put up with all the sin. I think God wants to see what we do. He gave us free will, so we have a choice. I know God is seeing lots of bad things happening on this earth. I feel bad that He sees the mess, and we are all to blame, since we are all sinners. Of course some people are worse than others. There are all kinds of people.

If we think about this perfect, and powerful God, and what people do, we can more understand the great flood you read about in the Bible. There weren't near as many people on earth during that flood, but God got wrathful from what He was seeing. It was His creation to get rid of if He wanted. He almost did. God told man, even given the rainbow as a reminder that He wouldn't wipe out man again.

Things are different now after the time of Jesus. We all have a choice.

This book is about God wanting to get our attention. It is not an easy thing to understand that God is really a part of us, and we are part of God. God knows us better than we do. God put the breath of life into all of us. Since He knows how many hairs you have on your head, He also knows how you are on the inside. The Bible says God looks into the heart.

Again, this book is about God wanting to get your attention. People are all different, and we live in a world that is not going to give God a lot of credit for all of it. Some people can see that God had to be responsible for everything and they love God.

God actually made it easy for us humans to know Him, and believe. Life isn't always easy for sure on this planet where there is a battle going on of good and bad, love and hate, and God and Satan. It is an invisible battle with us in the middle. I know many don't believe this, but they do believe in corona virus, that we also can't see. I know we can see it under a strong microscope. There are things out there that we can't see.

We can't really know or understand God. His being all-powerful and all-knowing is just amazing. He did give us a lot that we would know about Him. In God's Holy Word, the Bible, He wanted us to know certain things. God always seems to give us extra like creation, and the Bible. I mean extra by so much creation and life. The Bible gives us history, and so much more than the things God needed us to know. God needed us to know about His Son Jesus. He needed us to know that He has always loved us, and He needed us to know that He wants us to spend eternity with Him. We need to think of all those prophecies that God is responsible for, in the Bible. These prophecies prove God, and He put so many of them.

Creation was all for us to be with God forever. That brings up the problem of sin. God did right in giving His creation freedom, or free will. With the nudging by Satan we sinned. Man did exactly what God told him not to do. So, we can't be with a perfect God as sinners. God with His power, and knowledge, had to fix it because He loves us and wants those that will, to live with Him for eternity. We have many mysteries in our world, and one is that this all-powerful God is going to do what He planned. He fixed this sin problem through His Son

Jesus. The perfect world that God originally created, He will have again. So, God has done everything, and more for us to be able to be with Him. He is at work all the time trying to save as many of us as possible. He has many humans helping Him. They are His children. He is God the Father.

There are many good people on this planet that take everything for granted. They do what they need to do, take care of their family, and just live life. They don't think much about a Creator, God. We have every opportunity in this country to seek God. We were given free will from God. Our freedom first came from God. That is also why we had a great country, and still do. We put God first. The country is not as great as it used to be, and we should know why. Like it has always been, people get farther away from God. The Bible tells us if we don't seek the Creator, God, and believe in His Son Jesus, we won't get to spend eternity with God. Why wouldn't humans be interested in finding out about the Creator? That should be the main thing we do on this planet. Humans are curious, and we enjoy mysteries. All of this, and certainly ourselves is a mystery. We can always think we evolved from ape. Monkeys and all kinds of different apes are animals like all the rest.

All good people out there need to think. Yes, bad people also can spend eternity with God. Jesus didn't come to this earth, and die in our place for good sinners, or bad sinners. He died for all sinners. We are all sinners, some of us are certainly worse than others. Thinking of bad people, or sinners their problem is, they will likely not seek God. I pray for them, and all of us.

I'm going to mention more about the corona virus infecting our world. Well we have bad people infecting our world and using their virus to run our lives. We can understand those that are trying to keep us safe, but there are others that are hateful and mean, and in power. We have other countries that use things to run people's lives. There are many in our own country that want to run our lives. I've never understood why some people want power over others. I don't think I'm better or worse than anyone else. If I am better, it is thanks to God. He is the only one that can make us better. There are many out there that think they are better than others, because they have a lot of money, or more power. Some even think they are more religious, and so are closer to God. If we have different colored skin, or more money, or more power, or even more religion, we are all created the same and God loves us the same. Humans have always compared themselves to others. We should love God and do the best we can and help one another.

I have a small business, and even smaller now, since I work alone, and it is a needed business. So many people have businesses, and that is how the country thrives. I don't make a lot of money, and many people don't, but we are as important as anyone else. I can't understand why people want to even feel important. Speaking of being important, we are important to our families, but we are very important to God. Can you imagine why we are so important to God? For one thing God created us and loves us.

How people are, and how they act, and treat others has always been wondered about, or talked about. God gave man and woman freedom, or free will to be, and do as they please. We all have to admit that was the right thing to do. America followed God's will and built a country based on these freedoms. I touched on America in this book already, about what happened when we put God first. God gave us liberty, and freedom, America gave us the Bill of Rights, laws to go by, and a constitution. By putting God first America put itself on track to be great. Our Pledge of Allegiance says one nation under God, and our money says in God We Trust. Our country is actually more proof of God. He blessed this country. With everything we have now, everyone would have to say we have a pretty easy life. I mean all the conveniences; many get farther away from God. We have so much to keep us occupied. People do occasionally think of God, like after 9/11. When God is neglected things seems to get worse. After having such a blessed country, and we can live a pretty easy life, we don't have to consider anything else. That is true, we don't have to. We are living in a different time and we don't need God so much anymore. Is that true? Some have put God to the side. And some never think about Him. Some wonder if God still blesses America. God doesn't change like humans do. God blesses people. It is people that get away from God. Everything God has done for us, not to mention we walk on this planet because of God. How about God's Son Jesus, what He was sent to do for us? It is just nice that God is not like us humans. I'll just say we have some time. Who knows how much? The Bible says God will eventually make things like He did in the beginning. There will be no more sin, or death, or sorrow.

Many people in the world and the country put God first, and love God. They are not perfect, but they try, and they lean on God for help.

Think about our government that pushes hate, and if you don't think like them you are racist, or other words they like to use. Shame on them. It is all about the vote, but mostly their power. If our government looked to God, He would wonder where the love for fellow men, and country went. Our government must not think about us, the people. They live in their bubble in Washington. I know there is a small amount in government that tries.

The government and TV commercials seem to treat us like we are stupid. They are wrong. Our government has been hurting people for a long time. Americans have our own problems, but we have to do our job out here with that weight on our back, of knowing you, the government is ruining the country. It doesn't matter who is in power now, because the damage was done years ago. We can't pay the national debt, and we can't help you with all your hate and division. You are pushing all of this bad stuff from your bubble in Washington. The people are concerned with taking care of themselves and their families.

Things happen all the time on this earth that God created. Mostly things happen with humans. There is just so much to creation. In writing this book I think of things that I need to talk about for this book. My mother and I were given some pecans today. I looked at those pecans and thought of the huge variety of things God gave us to eat on this planet. All kinds of nuts. Then I thought about all the kinds of seasonings. All the seasonings is sure something we should thank God for. Only God could even imagine all these things. I think He gave us all these things because He can, and He cares about us. Again, most people just take all these things for granted.

If you were to make a list of everything on this planet, from big things to tiny things you would end up with volumes of pages. You still couldn't even think of them all.

Just thinking about all the different kinds of food, seasonings to cook with, and coffee, tea, chocolate, well the list goes on and on. This is all amazing and is here because we have an amazing God.

There are things in the Bible that we don't really understand. Humans can always seem to have some argument. Like is the universe billions of years old, or thousands of years old. I know Christians believe in billions of years, and some believe in thousands of years. The Bible doesn't give us a perfect answer to that question. Scientists also only use educated guesses to that question. I know the arguments. The rock layers, carbon dating, light from distant stars, and they tell us man evolved from ape. I have my ideas on how old the universe might be, but since the Bible doesn't tell us I'm not going to get into the argument. Some say the great flood could have changed the earth's whole landscape into looking much older. I do know that the world, and humans like to gripe, and the Bible, and God are things they gripe about. Instead of trying to prove these things, the Bible and God wrong, we should do it different and try to prove them right. If we try to prove them wrong, we are doing exactly what Satan wants us to do. If we try to prove them true and right we do what God would have us do.

God gave us a Bible to tell us things He wanted us to know. I mean things you can't get anywhere else. I believe humans have always guessed about creation and life or they believe in what the creator, God says. Some go out of their way to dispute the Bible and God. There is no way to figure out this all-powerful, all-knowing God. The ones of us that do believe are glad that God is a loving, and merciful God. I don't think God is very happy about what He sees happening on this planet.

How can people not see the plan to this world of ours? Think of all the things set up a certain way, and most of them needed to be set up in a certain way for life to exist. People don't think about it, or they take it for granted like I've said many times in the book. I could write on and on about little things, to big things that are all set up a certain way for life to exist on this planet. We even have things we didn't have to have, like the wildflowers. I think God does things like that, because He can, and He loves us.

I pray for everyone out there on this amazing earth, and hope you see this wonderful God, that is waiting for you.

God let us know what He wanted us to know, and that is all. Satan wants us to find reasons to rule out God and the Bible. Satan is anti-love and God is love.

Bible verses references:

Prophecies of the coming and death of Jesus.

Isaiah 7:14

Therefore, the Lord himself shall give you a sign; Behold, a virgin shall conceive, and bear a son, and shall call His name Immanuel.

Zachariah 9:9

Rejoice greatly, O daughter of Zion; shout, O daughter of Jerusalem: See your king comes to you righteous and victorious, lowly, and riding on a donkey, on a colt, the foal of a donkey.

Psalms 31:13

For I hear many whispering terrors on every side! They conspire against me and plot to take my life.

Isaiah 25:7-8

On this mountain He will destroy the shroud that enfolds all peoples, the sheets that covers all nations; He will swallow up death forever. The sovereign Lord will wipe away the tears from all faces; He will remove His peoples disgrace from on the earth. The Lord has spoken.

Psalms 22:16

Dogs surround me, a pack of villains incircle me; they pierced my hands and feet.

Psalm 22:7-8

All who see me make fun of me. Insults pour from their mouths. They shake their hands and say, put yourself in the Lord's hands. Let the Lord save Him! Let God rescue Him since He is pleased with Him!

Isaiah 53:5

He was wounded for our rebellious acts. He was crushed for our sins.

Matthew 24:35

The earth and heavens will disappear, but my words will never disappear.

Prophecies about Israel (the Jews return)

Amos 9:14-15 (written about 750 B.C.)

I will restore my people Israel. They will rebuild the ruined cities and live in them. They will plant vineyards and drink the wine from them. They will plant gardens and eat their fruit. I will plant the people of Israel in their land, and they won't be uprooted again from the land that I gave them, says the Lord your God.

Ezekiel 34:13 (written between 593-571 B.C.)

I will bring them out from the nations, gather them from the countries, and bring them to their own land. I will take care of them on the mountains of Israel, by the streams and in the inhabited places of land.

Leviticus 26:11-12

I will put my tent among you, and I will never look at you with disgust. So, I will live among you and be your God, and you will be my people.

Jeremiah 31:10

Hear the word of the Lord, you nations, listen to the word of the Lord. Tell it to the distant islands. Say, the one who scattered the people of Israel will gather them and watch over them as a shepherd watches over His flock. The Lord will free the descendants of Jacob and reclaim them from those who are stronger than they are.

God and His prophecies.

Isaiah 46:8-14

Remember this, and take courage. Recall your rebellious acts. Remember the first events, because I am God, and there is no other. I am God, and there's no one like me. From the beginning I revealed the end. From long ago I told you things that had not yet happened, saying, My plan will stand, and I'll do everything I intended to do. I will call a bird of prey from the east. I will call someone for my plan from a faraway land. I have spoken, and I will bring it about, I have planned it, and I will do it.

Isaiah 42:8-9

I am the Lord; that is my name. I will not give my glory to anyone else or the praise I deserved to idols. What I said in the past has come true. I will reveal new things before they happen.

Jeremiah 9:23-24

This is what the Lord says: don't let wise people brag about their wisdom. Don't let strong people brag about their strength. Don't let rich people brag about their riches. If they want to brag, they should brag that they understand and know Me. They should brag that I, the Lord, act out of love, righteousness, and justice on earth. This kind of bragging pleases me, declares the Lord.

Hebrews 11:6

No one can please God without faith. Whoever goes to God must believe that God exists and that He rewards those who seek him.

Ecclesiastics 11:5

Just as you don't know how the breath of life enters the limbs of a child in its mother's womb, you also don't understand how God who made everything, works.

1 John 4:7-9

Dear friends, let us love one another, for love comes from God. Whoever does not love does not know God, because God is love. This is how God showed His love among us: He sent His one and only Son into the world that we might live through Him.